Cambridge Elements

Elements in Theatre, Performance and the Political
edited by
Trish Reid
University of Reading
Liz Tomlin
University of Glasgow

PERFORMANCE AND POSTSOCIALISM IN POSTMILLENNIAL CHINA

Rossella Ferrari
University of Vienna, Austria

Shaftesbury Road, Cambridge CB2 8EA, United Kingdom

One Liberty Plaza, 20th Floor, New York, NY 10006, USA

477 Williamstown Road, Port Melbourne, VIC 3207, Australia

314–321, 3rd Floor, Plot 3, Splendor Forum, Jasola District Centre, New Delhi – 110025, India

103 Penang Road, #05–06/07, Visioncrest Commercial, Singapore 238467

Cambridge University Press is part of Cambridge University Press & Assessment, a department of the University of Cambridge.

We share the University's mission to contribute to society through the pursuit of education, learning and research at the highest international levels of excellence.

www.cambridge.org
Information on this title: www.cambridge.org/9781009515894

DOI: 10.1017/9781009515900

First published 2025

A catalogue record for this publication is available from the British Library

ISBN 978-1-009-51589-4 Hardback
ISBN 978-1-009-51594-8 Paperback
ISSN 2753-1244 (online)
ISSN 2753-1236 (print)

Performance and Postsocialism in Postmillennial China

Elements in Theatre, Performance and the Political

DOI: 10.1017/9781009515900
First published online: January 2025

Rossella Ferrari
University of Vienna, Austria

Author for correspondence: Rossella Ferrari, rossella.ferrari@univie.ac.at

Abstract: This Element examines performance in postmillennial China through the lens of postsocialism. The fragmented ontology of Chinese postsocialism captures the contradictions of a political system supporting a neoliberal economy while continuing to promote socialist values. The Element explores how the ideological ambivalence and cultural paradoxes characterising the postsocialist condition are reflected in performance. Focusing on independent practitioners and postdramatic practices, it builds on theorisations of postsocialism as a state of temporal disjunction to propose a tripartite taxonomy structured around past, present, and future temporal regimes. Categories of *postsocialist hauntologies*, *postsocialist realisms*, and *postsocialist futurities* are introduced to investigate performances that revisit the socialist past, document present realities, and envision future imaginations. The intersection of competing temporalities and their performative manifestations mirrors the disjunctive constitution of contemporary China, where socialist legacies and futurological ambitions coexist within a fractured postsocialist present. This title is also available as Open Access on Cambridge Core.

Keywords: Chinese theatre, Chinese performance cultures, postsocialism, postsocialist performance, postsocialist temporalities

ISBNs: 9781009515894 (HB), 9781009515948 (PB), 9781009515900 (OC)
ISSNs: 2753-1244 (online), 2753-1236 (print)

Contents

Introduction: Performing Postsocialist Times

Contemporary performance cultures offer a distinctive response to China's postsocialist zeitgeist. The transition from a planned to a market economy in the late twentieth century has profoundly redefined the cultural politics, creative practices, and production conditions of performance. As with other areas of Chinese postsocialist culture, the performing arts have expanded and diversified in the new millennium, witnessing a multiplicity of stylistic approaches, thematic orientations, and production models, and the consolidation of a vigorous independent scene. Postsocialist performance reverberates with the dissonant affective structures that define Chinese postsocialism as a protracted transitional state of both continuity and rupture with historical legacies and ideological formations (Lu, 2007; Zhang, 2008). This Element therefore aims to assess the impact of postsocialism, as both a theoretical construct and a concrete lived experience, on the practice and politics of performance and on the formulation of new concepts, aesthetics, and critical perspectives, drawing attention to postsocialist conditions that have catalysed shifts in artistic production and discourse since the turn of the millennium.

I approach postsocialist performance through a temporal lens, clustering my inquiry around three distinct, yet overlapping, regimes of past, present, and future temporalities. This framework aligns with theorisations of Chinese postsocialism as a heterogeneous and temporally disjointed cultural phenomenon (Lu, 2007; Berry, 2009). The rationale for adopting temporal regimes as the organising principle of this study stems from the observation that China's postmillennial performance ecologies resonate with three aesthetic and discursive modalities, or dispositions, that together capture the constitutive heterochrony of postsocialism. These modalities illuminate the aesthetic enactment of the disjunctive ontology of postsocialism and the entanglements of experiential reality with the politics of embodiment and representation. The interplay of temporal regimes and their performative manifestations – or, *performances of postsocialist times* – reflects the socioeconomic asymmetries and dissonant cultural formations that have surfaced in the Chinese public sphere since the acceleration of the communist party-state's reformist agenda in the late twentieth century and the country's emergence as a global economic power in the new millennium.

To explore the nexus of performance and postsocialism, Section 1 traces the convergence of theories of Chinese postsocialism and configurations of postsocialist performance. It frames the analysis around the activities of independent practitioners and emerging postdramatic practices as symptomatic aesthetic responses to China's postmillennial condition, where the interrogation of the incongruities of postsocialism has been most pronounced. I propose a temporal taxonomy structured around the conceptual categories of *postsocialist hauntologies*, *postsocialist realisms*, and *postsocialist futurities*. These categories respectively foreground productions that revive the spectral remains of the socialist past (Section 2), record current social realities (Section 3), and project futural scenarios (Section 4). This tripartite structure mirrors the fragmented sociocultural fabric of twenty-first-century China, where past socialist legacies and futurological ambitions cohabit a disjointed postsocialist present. The reverberations of postsocialist temporal regimes in postmillennial independent performance are assessed through the work of Wen Hui and the Living Dance Studio, Wang Chong and Théâtre du Rêve Expérimental, Li Jianjun and the New Youth Group, Li Ning and the Physical Guerrillas, Grass Stage, and Wang Mengfan. The Conclusion reflects on the transnational ramifications of Chinese postsocialism as manifested in performance beyond China's borders, through the practice of American artist Jen Liu.

1 Postsocialism and Postsocialist Performance

1.1 Chinese Postsocialism

Postsocialism has been a prominent concept in academic discourse on China since the late twentieth century. Arif Dirlik first invoked the term in 1989 to rationalise the Chinese Communist Party's (CCP) ambiguous formulation of 'socialism with Chinese characteristics' (*Zhongguo tese shehui zhuyi*) as the new guiding ideology of the People's Republic of China (PRC) in the post-Mao era. The death of Mao Zedong (1893–1976) sealed the end of a decade of ideological radicalism and severe social disruption during the Cultural Revolution (1966–76). In the early 1980s, the reforms spearheaded by Deng Xiaoping (1904–97) ushered in a new era of economic marketisation, social modernisation, and cultural liberalisation under the slogan 'reform and opening up' (*gaige kaifang*). Writing before the collapse of the Soviet Union, the disintegration of the Eastern Bloc, and the political crisis caused by the 1989 Tiananmen Square democracy movement – all pivotal events that would reconfigure China's political economy and postsocialism itself – Dirlik sought to describe an embryonic 'condition of ideological contradiction and uncertainty'. This condition arose from a waning faith in socialism 'as a metatheory of politics' on the one hand and, on the other, as 'a response to the experience of capitalism' (1989: 34). A few years later, Paul Pickowicz redefined Chinese postsocialism in cultural terms to describe the alienated 'popular perception' (1994: 61) of socialism as reflected in 1980s urban cinema. Pickowicz argues that an inherently cynical, if not outright 'dystopian', postsocialist condition emerges whenever 'popular faith in socialism has vanished, but the economic, political, and cultural legacies of the traditional socialist era continue to have a profound influence on daily social life' (62). The conceptual framework of postsocialism has since gained traction and been widely applied in studies of Chinese literature, media, and visual culture. However, there has been little reflection on the concept within theatre and performance studies, nor has there been a comprehensive examination of the new performance cultures that have developed since the onset of the postsocialist era through the prism of postsocialism. This study begins to bridge this gap by assessing the cultural, political, and aesthetic implications of *performing postsocialism* in postmillennial China.

The postsocialist turn has been theorised from various critical perspectives and definitions. In a study of postsocialist cinema, Zhang Yingjin summarises the discourse in four categories: 'postsocialism as a label of historical periodization; postsocialism as a structure of feelings; postsocialism as a set of aesthetic practices; and postsocialism as a regime of political economy' (2007: 50). Some scholars trace the origins of Chinese postsocialism as a periodising category to the late 1970s and 1980s (Dirlik, 1989; Pickowicz, 1994; Berry, 2004). Most, however, see the early reform period or New Era (*xin shiqi*) as merely a prelude to a full-fledged postsocialist condition emerging in the 1990s with the acceleration of Deng's blueprint for a socialist market economy in the aftermath of the 1989 Tiananmen Square crackdown (Lu, 2007; McGrath, 2008; Zhang, 2008). Economic restructuring radically reconfigured social relations, stimulating 'marketization', 'pluralization', 'individualization', and 'differentiation' in the cultural and creative industries (McGrath, 2008: 7). 'Compared to the previous decade of Chinese reforms', Zhang Xudong notes, 'the post-Tiananmen growth and prosperity were accompanied by a very different historical tension, urgency, and anxiety, which in turn gave rise to a very different mode of perception, expression, and representation' (2008: 7). This rupture became more pronounced with the PRC's entry into the World Trade Organisation in 2001 (Lu, 2007: 208) and its repositioning as a global economic power in the new millennium, leading to even newer cultural perceptions, expressions, and representations.

Postsocialism encapsulates an ambiguous historical condition and affective structure of residuality, liminality, and transience, as remnants of traditional ethics and ideologies coexist with new globalised values and behaviours. As such, it echoes Raymond Williams's notion of the structure of feeling as a fluid discursive formation that 'appears in the gap between the official discourse of policy and regulations, the popular response to official discourse and its appropriation in literary and other cultural texts' (Buchanan, 2018). Structures of feeling connect to the realm of perception as dynamic affective trajectories and 'ways of thinking vying to emerge at any one time in history', as Ian Buchanan observes, reflecting the dominant spirit of the time. Similarly, Sheldon Lu describes Chinese postsocialism as a 'cultural logic' that 'negotiate[s] the residual socialist past and the emergent capitalist present to concoct new imaginaries of a transitional society' (2007: 208). Postsocialist culture articulates this transitional logic through a spectrum of aesthetic modes and affective moods that resonate in postsocialist (post-Soviet, post-communist) contexts elsewhere (see Erjavec, 2003), ranging from alienation, resistance, and denial to cynicism, parody, and nostalgia. However, China stands out among post-socialist societies for its active participation in the global neoliberal economy while officially retaining socialism as the nation's guiding political ideology under the one-party rule of the CCP.

While acknowledging the specificity of the Chinese experience, postsocialism has been linked to global theories of 'uneven' (Gong, 2012) and 'capitalist' modernity (McGrath, 2008), and described as a local variation of postmodernism (Lu, 2007; Zhang, 2008; Berry, 2009). As 'the cultural logic of late capitalism' (Jameson, 1991), postmodernism harbours 'incredulity toward metanarratives' (Lyotard, 1984: xxiv). Similarly, as the cultural logic of late or residual socialism, postsocialism counters the grand narratives of socialist modernity with 'a set of alternative aesthetic practices' (Zhang, 2007: 51) that break from the ideological totality and relative uniformity of socialist culture to embrace a pluralised culture of fragments (McGrath, 2008: 22–24). Just as postmodernism exhibits 'time-space compression' and the 'superimposition of different ontological worlds' (Harvey, 1989: 50), postsocialism manifests 'unevenness' (Gong, 2012: 1), and 'disjuncture' (Lu, 2007: 138), as well as continuities with the Mao era (1949–76) – hence a simultaneous critique of and nostalgia for socialism.

Postsocialism 'as a regime of political economy' (Zhang, 2007: 50) coincides with the rise of Chinese postmodernism in the post-1989 period, or Post-New Era (*hou xinshiqi*) (Lu, 2007; Zhang, 2008). The 1990s saw the emergence of distinctly postmodernist phenomena, such as the narrowing of the gap between high and low culture through the depoliticisation of an increasingly commodified cultural field; the substitution of the modernist cultural production of the previous decade with parody, pastiche, and language games; 'the alienation of the subject' superseded by its 'fragmentation' (Jameson, 1991: 14); symptoms of Maoist nostalgia; and political numbness and cynicism in the wake of profound national trauma. This hybrid regime emerges from mixed feelings of anxiety and expectation generated by deepening ideological contradictions and socioeconomic segmentation in the present, combined with prefigurations of unfulfilled scenarios and dormant possibilities from the past that linger into the future. Undoubtedly, the postsocialist transformation of Chinese society has led to a widening class divide and rampant economic inequality. Yet, the postsocialist turn has also spurred cultural autonomy and artistic diversity through the expansion of the creative economy, fostering distinctive cultural politics and aesthetic formations. This tension between the anxieties and potentials of the present resonates with Dirlik's take on postsocialism as an opportunity to reconsider the experience of socialism – and its cultural and artistic remnants – 'in new, more creative ways' (1989: 43).

The advent of postsocialism did not sound the death knell of socialism. Rather, it announced the inception of a residual cultural phenomenon resulting from 'a bewildering overlap of modes of production, social systems, and symbolic orders, all of which lay claim to a fledgling world of life' (Zhang, 2008: 10). The prefix 'post' does not indicate the 'beyond' or 'after' of socialism in a strict chronological sense, not least because the PRC is still nominally a socialist state. It denotes a moment of interchange; not a definitive end, but the prospect of new beginnings. As the artistic works examined in this study illustrate, the 'post' of postsocialist performance underscores a tension between the pursuit of the new and a lingering apprehension, or sometimes even a subcutaneous nostalgia, for the old. As Lu notes, however, postsocialist nostalgia does not simply yearn for a re-enactment of the past; or, in Svetlana Boym's terms, it is not a purely 'retrospective' form of 'restorative nostalgia'. Rather, it echoes Boym's 'prospective' mode of 'reflective nostalgia' (2001: xvi). It is a nostalgia that revisits the past not only as it was but as it might have been, or as it might have been differently, and that moves towards yet inactivated prospects and future-oriented scenarios (Lu, 2007: 132). The palimpsestic ontology of postsocialism presupposes a heterochronic space in which both remnants of traditional ways of life and their neoliberal post-lives unfold and intertwine. As it turns away from the socialist past, Chinese postsocialism both contains and negotiates socialism ideologically, culturally, affectively, and aesthetically.

1.2 Performing Chinese Postsocialism

Having traced the conceptual trajectory and distinctive features of Chinese postsocialism according to Zhang Yingjin's four categories, I will now recast these categories within the specific setting of postsocialist performance to define the scope and key concerns of my analysis.

With regard to 'postsocialism as a label of historical periodization' (2007: 50), this study examines postmillennial performance cultures against the backdrop of sociopolitical reconfigurations in postsocialist China during the same period. The years leading up to the 2008 Beijing Summer Olympics and the inauguration of Xi Jinping's leadership in 2013 represent two critical junctures for both postsocialist society and performance as, respectively, a moment of innovation, internationalisation, and creative exuberance, and one of nationalist conservatism and inward-looking closure. The Xi era has ushered in a new phase of postsocialist authoritarianism while also redefining the relationship between past, present, and future (Lanza, 2023: 608). The principle of socialism with Chinese characteristics, which paved the way for a market economy and sparked the debate on Chinese postsocialism in the 1980s, has been inscribed in the new ideological orthodoxy known as the 'Xi Jinping Thought on Socialism with Chinese Characteristics for a New Era', enshrined in the CCP Constitution in 2017. The Core Socialist Values (*shehui zhuyi hexin jiazhiguan*), formulated in 2006 and revived in 2012, and Xi's signature doctrine of the Chinese Dream (*Zhongguo meng*), introduced in 2012 and formalised in 2013 as a vision of 'the great rejuvenation of the Chinese nation' (*Zhonghua minzu weida fuxing*), have become integral to the CCP's official narratives in the new millennium. This rhetorical arsenal has taken centre stage in the political performances of an increasingly autocratic leadership, engaged in a perpetual and almost paranoid quest for persuasive 'dramaturgic imagery' (Strauss, 2021: 407) and 'unifying scripts' (408).[1]

Xi's rejuvenation plan for twenty-first-century China does not only celebrate the modern past defined by Maoism. In contrast to the socialist-era condemnation of traditional cultures as regressive and reactionary, and with much greater emphasis than Xi's predecessors, the rhetorical armoury of the Chinese Dream discourse has also revisited imageries and scripts from the nation's imperial past to construct optimistic visions of the future (Miao, 2021: 162). This resurgence of traditional values and national cultural heritage is central to the CCP's public communication strategies. The Core Socialist Values and the Chinese Dream have been the subject of official ceremonials, visual propaganda campaigns (Miao, 2021), and state-sponsored song-and-dance performances (Zhao, 2016). While these phenomena are beyond the purview of this study, they constitute a significant dimension of performing postsocialism in postmillennial China.

The phrase *performing postsocialism* captures two facets of the nexus of performance and postsocialism that guides my inquiry, as well as two discrete articulations of what I designate as performances of postsocialist times. First, postsocialism can be understood as a subject that performs itself, and second, as an object that is being performed or is enacted through performance. One accounts for the performative aspects of postsocialist sociopolitical praxis, and the other for performance praxis produced under postsocialist sociopolitical

[1] The Core Socialist Values include four national values (prosperity, democracy, civility, harmony), four social values (freedom, equality, justice, rule of law), and four personal values (patriotism, dedication, integrity, friendliness) (Miao, 2021: 167).

conditions. Although the boundaries between these definitions can be porous and dependent on framing and interpretation, the former takes an expanded approach to performance and performativity. Resonating with Richard Schechner's *is/as* criterion (2013: 38), it encompasses a broad spectrum of practices that can be framed *as* performance, while the latter points to a narrower definition of an entity that *is* performance; in this case, artistic productions.

In light of this distinction, *postsocialism as a subject that performs itself* denotes a non-artistic process by which postsocialism, as both a socioeconomic regime and a cultural condition, has been enacted at official and unofficial levels since the reform era. This perspective would include the study of mass spectacles and mega-events that serve as platforms for performances of national identity and cultural nationalism, such as the 2010 World Expo in Shanghai and the 2008 and 2022 Olympic Games in Beijing. The choreographed exhibitions and elaborate ceremonials on display at these events showcased postsocialist China as a powerful actor and rising star on the international stage. This framework would also consider institutional practices and state rituals that political scientists have studied through the lens of performance. These range from theatricalised gestures of 'performative governance' (Ding, 2022: 6) to meticulously scripted acts such as formal speeches, meetings, public appearances, and other ritualised repertoires through which the (post)socialist state ensures its legitimacy and stability (Strauss, 2021). It would also explore 'counterscripts' (408) and 'contentious performances' (Tilly, 2008), such as demonstrations, protests, and performances of political activism, together with vernacular dramaturgies of daily life, practices of leisure, and everyday performances of resistance and survival. Life under state socialism has often been framed in terms of 'social mimesis' (Pang, 2017: 10), portraying citizens as simultaneously actors and spectators in a public national drama. The performative properties of state governance and social behaviour persist in the postmillennial afterlife of socialism, to the extent that the cultural logic of postsocialist China itself could be seen *as* a culture of performance. Indeed, the phenomenon of social performativity is not unique to China, nor to socialist or postsocialist societies. But the distinctive confluence of the new dynamics of postsocialist neoliberalism and the residues of socialist authoritarianism – with its persisting demands for ideological conformity to the diktats of the party-state – arguably makes this aspect more pronounced.

Postsocialism as an object that is being performed refers instead to creative endeavours within the artistic realm that articulate and are themselves symptomatic of the postsocialist zeitgeist as enacted, embodied, and represented through performance; in other words, performances of and about 'postsocialism as a structure of feelings', according to Zhang's schema (2007: 50). It is this latter understanding of the convergence of performance and postsocialism that forms the core of my inquiry. The postmillennium has produced a plethora of aesthetic responses to the ambiguities of postsocialism, to the economic and existential effects of this incongruous condition on performance practice, and to its multifaceted reverberations in the realms of the social, the political, and the affective, resonating more acutely within the independent ecosystem that has grown alongside the larger state-sponsored and commercial mainstream. This dimension of performing postsocialism aligns with Zhang's characterisation of postsocialism 'as a set of alternative aesthetic practices' (51). Here, 'alternative' signifies both an independent *position* at a structural and systemic level and a critical *disposition* towards experimentation in content, style, and form.

On one level, the independent performance practices discussed in this study can be described as alternative because their channels of production and circulation are positioned on the margins of the nationwide network of state institutions and infrastructures (companies, academies, venues, human resources) that has been in place since the early 1950s – itself a legacy of the socialist past that persists in the postsocialist present. Many of these institutions have been reformed or merged into larger media and arts conglomerates as part of a wider restructuring of the state sector since the advent of the market economy, and continue to occupy a prominent position in the national performing arts ecosystem. Furthermore, these alternative practices resist the encroachment of the commercial establishment, which has flourished in consequence of the government's promotion of the cultural and creative industries and the privatisation of performing arts enterprises. They are largely independent of mainstream markets and state-sponsored funding schemes, which typically demand conformity to official themes and values.[2] As such, both practitioners and practices are commonly described as operating 'outside the system' (*tizhi wai*; i.e., independently) as opposed to 'inside the system' (*tizhi nei;* i.e., within the state infrastructure). At the same time, the permeable margin between 'outside' (*wai*) and 'inside' (*nei*) – that is, negotiations between independent and institutional, marginal and mainstream positions – and the growing convergence of state and commercial forces within the mainstream are also defining features of the postmillennial performing arts landscape.

On another level, these practices offer an aesthetic alternative to the stylistic norms and ideological values embedded in state-orchestrated public spectacles, the conservative repertoire of state-run theatres, and profit-driven entertainment, as

[2] For example, the China National Arts Fund (Guojia yishu jijin), a government scheme launched in 2013, supports art that 'serves the people and socialism' and 'contributes to building a socialist cultural power', according to its website (https://www.cnaf.cn/single_detail/105.html).

practitioners navigate political sensitivities while pushing the boundaries of generic and representational conventions. With few exceptions, most of the artists discussed in this study emerged in Beijing and Shanghai, China's largest cities and cultural epicentres. Most belong to a cohort of experimentalists who entered the scene in the first decade of the twenty-first century and have gained national and international recognition since the second. Many have been associated with independent creative spaces and communities, such as Beijing's CCD Workstation (Caochangdi gongzuozhan) and Shanghai's Downstream Garage (Xiahe micang) – both inaugurated in 2005 and closed in 2013 and 2014 respectively. They have also found support through platforms such as the Beijing Fringe Festival (Beijing qingnian yishu jie; est. 2008), the Penghao Theatre's (Penghao juchang) Nanluoguxiang Performing Arts Festival (Nanluoguxiang xiju jie; est. 2010), also in Beijing, and incubators for emerging artists at international festivals in Beijing, Shanghai, Wuzhen, and elsewhere. Notable groups include Grass Stage (Caotaiban), the Niao Collective (Zuheniao), Xiao Ke x Zihan, Li Ning's Physical Guerrillas (Lingyun yan zhiti youjidui), Li Jianjun's New Youth Group (Xin qingnian jutuan), Wang Chong's Théâtre du Rêve Expérimental (Xinchuan shiyan jutuan), and Wang Mengfan's Walking Theatre (Xingzou juchang). Influential figures from the premillennial generation of postsocialist experimentalists, such as Zhang Xian, Tian Gebing's Paper Tiger Theatre Studio (Zhi laohu xiju gongzuoshi), and Wen Hui's Living Dance Studio (Shenghuo wudao gongzuoshi), continue to operate independently into the twenty-first century.

Moreover, postmillennial independent performance illustrates the productive intersection between the 'post' of postsocialism in cultural theory and the 'post' of postdramatic in artistic practice. Particularly since the 2010 Chinese translation of Hans-Thies Lehmann's *Postdramatic Theatre* (2006, originally published in German in 1999), many independent practitioners, including those discussed in this study, have recognised the postdramatic – alongside its indigenous conceptual kin, *juchang* (performance-based theatre, see Section 1.4) – as fitting descriptors for their institutional position and artistic disposition within the domestic performing arts landscape (Li Y., 2019 and 2021; Tuchmann, 2022). While the 'post' of postsocialism is often aligned with the 'post' of postmodernism in theories of premillennial postsocialist arts and cultures, it intersects significantly with the 'post' of postdramatic in postmillennial performance discourse. The postdramatic has emerged as a marker of divergence from both the values of commercial and state-sponsored cultural industries and the practices of earlier generations of postsocialist experimentalists. Thus, the dual focus of this study lies on postmillennial postsocialism in terms of historical periodisation – namely, the reconfiguration of Chinese postsocialism since the twenty-first century – and on postdramatic performance as one of its principal artistic manifestations.

With regard to Zhang's fourth categorisation, 'postsocialism as a regime of political economy' (2007: 50), analysing postsocialism through the lens of performance and vice versa sheds light on the interconnections between the arts, state politics, and economic development. The neoliberal policies of marketisation, privatisation, mass entrepreneurship, and innovation promoted by the state within the cultural and creative industries, including the performing arts (see Li, 2022), have opened new channels for independent producers, but also closed off others. This is especially true for the noncommercial and ideologically nonaligned forms of performance that are the subject of this research. For these, the stakes have been raised since Xi's leadership and under the draconian restrictions imposed during the COVID-19 pandemic, which only eased after unprecedented popular remonstrations during the highly performative White Paper Revolution (*baizhi geming*; or White Paper Movement, *baizhi yundong*) of late November 2022. Politics (propaganda, censorship, official approval) and capital (the commodification of the sector) are the two main vectors of state intervention in the performing arts. Despite the insistence of many foreign commentators on the former (the overused media binary of Chinese artists as being either oppressed or complicit with an authoritarian regime), it is the latter that has become an increasingly pressing concern for independent practitioners. Better still, the main challenge lies in the confluence of 'the powers of capitalism and political control', as dance artist Wen Hui has noted (Lee *et al.*, 2022: 285). Regardless of their self-positioning along the institutional-independent spectrum, all practitioners must navigate – and to varying degrees are entangled in – the collusion of state and capital that shapes the realities of performance production under postsocialist conditions. Undoubtedly, although beyond the scope of this study, a parallel assessment of the impact of postsocialist ideological and economic dynamics on the state-sanctioned and commercial mainstream, as an organic component of the contemporary performing arts environment, would further enhance our appreciation of the multiple meanings and manifestations of performing postsocialism in postmillennial China.

To conclude this preliminary categorisation, I supplement Zhang's fourfold typology with a fifth variation, postsocialism as a temporal regime – or, more precisely, a palimpsest of overlapping regimes of temporality – as an additional taxonomic descriptor that defines both the postsocialist condition and its performances.

1.3 Temporalities of Postsocialist Performance

Yan Lianke's *Lenin's Kisses* (Shouhuo), published in Chinese in 2004, begins with a masterful description of the experience of postsocialist time. A biting satire on the Disneyfication of socialism as a consumer attraction in a remote Chinese village, the novel portrays time in a state of 'temporal infirmity':

> During that year's sweltering summer, time fell out of joint. It became insane, even downright mad. Overnight, everything degenerated into disorder and lawlessness. And then it began to snow. Indeed, time itself fell ill. It went mad. (Yan, 2012: 3)

The eccentric community of disabled performers at the centre of Yan's narrative is a relic of bygone social structures and ways of life. Their village has survived political upheaval and economic transformation in a state of spatial seclusion and temporal suspension from conventional notions of historical time. This parallel social order is darkly symptomatic of the absurdities and competing ideological (dis)orders of contemporary China, where even the prospect of purchasing and profiting from the embalmed corpse of Vladimir Lenin seems perfectly reasonable (until it is not). The temporal malady affecting this society bespeaks the hauntological disjointedness of postsocialism as '*a queer temporality*' (Atanasoski and Vora, 2018: 141), which unsettles both the utopian teleology of accelerated progress that typifies the Maoist project of socialist modernity and the linear temporal logic of capitalist modernity.

Heterogeneous time is widely recognised as a hallmark of Chinese postsocialism, reflecting the coevalness of different stages of socioeconomic development and the resulting interpenetration of conflicting ideological regimes. Sheldon Lu identifies 'the coexistence of multiple temporalities' as a defining feature of the 'hyphenated construction' of postsocialist China, infused with 'nostalgia for the revolutionary past even as it enters the doors of the supermarket of capitalism' (2007: 210). Similarly, Chris Berry registers 'a variety of different temporalities in circulation' in postsocialist Chinese cinema (2009: 113), distinguishing between the 'future perfect tense' of the socialist era (115), the 'in-the-now temporality' of the present (117), and 'an uneasy in-the-now (and then) that invokes history and questions the present' (113). Postsocialism captures the multi-layered social spaces, hybrid technologies, and ideological overlaps that characterise China's contemporary reality, where past, present, and future dimensions collide and coexist within one another. As such, it reveals a set of discursive and aesthetic tendencies, or dispositions, shaped by distinct temporal modalities. These modalities blend the disjunctive 'in-the-now' of the present with practices, events, and imaginaries that extend forward and backward in time along a heterochronic spectrum that destabilises the seamlessly progressivist tempo of the nation-state's official chronographs. Echoing more widely studied articulations in Chinese literary, media, and visual cultures, Chinese performance cultures manifest postsocialist reality as both a ghostly reminder of the past and a forward-looking projection. Presocialist and socialist legacies linger as residues, ruins, and spectral revenants in the artistic enactments of the present, while simultaneously informing future-oriented visions and sensibilities.

Felipe Torres defines a *regime* as 'a predominant pattern for general process and activities' (2021: 25), and *temporal regimes* as 'diverse manifestations of time' or 'temporal varieties'. (3) Accordingly, my analysis frames postsocialism as a composite temporality constituted by overlapping manifestations of time. I adopt a temporal framework for categorising postsocialist performance to draw attention to the effects that the dissonant temporal varieties of Chinese postsocialism bear on the aesthetisation of this regime in artistic processes and activities. A temporal perspective highlights correspondences between the overlapping temporal regimes of postsocialism and the artistic regimes of embodiment and representation of a liminal relationship to the experience of time, clustered around specific moments in the past, present, and future. Each temporal manifestation determines the predominant aesthetic pattern and affective disposition of a specific performance, capturing an experience of reality that is also perceived as incongruous, stratified, and fragmented. As a temporal regime, postsocialism foregrounds 'heterochronies' – other or different 'slices in time' (Foucault, 1986: 26) – corresponding to the heterotopic intersection of rural and urban, industrial and post-industrial, 'premodern, modern, and postmodern' socio-aesthetic spaces (Lu, 2007: 153). Heterochronic time is neither unified nor complete, but rather accounts 'for a decentralised, pluriversal and multiple experience of time' (Torres, 2021: 3). It points to a relationship with time that deviates from the sense of closure and coherent progression embedded in the official temporalities and 'master futurologies of modernity' of the Chinese nation-state (Riemenschnitter *et al.*, 2022: 5). It is a time of palimpsestic interplay, punctuated by discrepancies, tensions, and frictions.

Likewise, postsocialist performance articulates a politics of time that captures the heterochronic experience of a protracted moment of historical suspension and socioeconomic unevenness. It incubates the capacity to disrupt conventional paradigms by drawing attention to 'break-experiences of time or "crises of time"' (Torres, 2021: 33), which counter the official temporality of 'progress, utopia and acceleration' (22). Equally crucial to conceptualising temporalities of postsocialist performance and, conversely, performances of postsocialist times, is Torres's view of temporal regimes as 'dispositions and dominant frames of understanding' (8). This suggests that a framework centred on regimes and politics of time can elucidate key aspects of the cultural manifestations of a specific era. Torres's framework supports the adoption of a temporal taxonomy in this study to understand the dominant dispositions and 'reiterative patterns'

(22) articulated through performance at particular points in time; in other words, the dominant structures of feeling that determine the selection of dramaturgical material and the aesthetic treatment of that material.

Accordingly, the following three sections each emphasise a dominant conceptual category and temporal modality of postsocialist performance. Performances of *postsocialist hauntologies*, *postsocialist realisms*, and *postsocialist futurities* are each distinguished by a spectrological engagement with the socialist past, a documentary inclination to record reality in the present moment, and a future-oriented sensibility – often, but not exclusively, articulated through technology. At the same time, this taxonomy accounts for tensions and dialectical interactions between these three modalities as tendencies or dispositions, rather than prescriptive classifications, which can accommodate performances of 'in-between times' (9). Thus, it resonates with the ontological constitution of Chinese postsocialism as 'an expectant present moment of unprecedented social experimentation that looks in two directions – back to the past and forward to the future' (Lu, 2007: 210). There is no finite dimension of time in postsocialism, but an incessant present continuous that contains a past (im)perfect and a future anterior; one that looks ahead (*post*) and *ante* (before, back).

1.4 Postsocialist Postdramatics: Independent Performance and *Juchang*

The Chinese term *juchang* captures the convergence of the 'post' of postsocialism with the 'post' of postdramatic, epitomising both a significant expression of postmillennial postsocialist performance and a local adaptation within the global discourse of postdramatic theatre. In discussing the postdramatic turn in theatre and performance since the late twenty-first century, Marvin Carlson argues that the terminological-conceptual redefinition implied by the prefix 'post' signals not only a quest for novelty against the status quo, but also a critical intention to break with its perceived stagnation (2015: 578). Andy Lavender further explores the cultural and political meanings of 'post' in light of shifts in the theorisation of (post)postmodernism and postdramatic performance under twenty-first-century neoliberal conditions. Echoing what I noted earlier in relation to the postness of postsocialism, Lavender argues that '[t]he term suggests an anxiety (or else, an urgency) to do with historical shift, nomenclatural definition and segmentation, and the tracing of cultural process'. This urgency intensifies with the intensification of changes in society and the economy (2019: 9), as has indeed been the case in postsocialist China. The embrace of the postdramatic as a preferred mode of independent performance, and as an alternative to the long-standing national tradition of text-based representational drama, testifies to a comparable concern for nomenclatural distinction and a corresponding urge for critical self-repositioning in relation to dominant artistic conventions and broader socio-economic and political reconfigurations in the twenty-first century. In both postsocialism and the postdramatic, the prefix serves as a temporal marker that also denotes a distinct structure of feeling.

The endorsement of *juchang*, which loosely translates as 'performance-based theatre', testifies to this affinity with the postdramatic framework. *Juchang* can be understood as a localised approach to the theory and practice of postdramatic theatre as introduced by Lehmann, which 'has thus become the central term of resonance of the postdramatic in China', as Kai Tuchmann notes (2022: 23). The term itself, however, is not new. *Juchang* literally means 'theatre', both as an art form and as the venue where it takes place. Related theoretical reflections can be traced back to earlier periods in Chinese theatre history. In the post-Mao era, for example, the distinction between *juchangxing* (theatricality) and *xijuxing* (dramaticality) outlined by playwright Gao Xingjian (1988) in a series of writings from the 1980s resonates in many ways with more recent conceptualisations of *juchang* through Lehmann's framework. Its twenty-first-century redefinition as an 'amplification of postdramatic thought' (Tuchmann, 2022: 23) stems from the distinction between the Chinese terms *xiju* and *juchang* introduced by scholar and practitioner Li Yinan in her translation of Lehmann's volume (2010). Li translates drama as *xiju* and theatre as *juchang,* thus rendering postdramatic theatre as *houxiju juchang*, where *hou* means 'post'. In her interpretation, *xiju* designates a text- and author-centric notion of dramatic theatre (*xiju juchang*), which is rooted in reproducibility and representational theatricality. In contrast, *juchang* refers to postdramatic, performance-based forms of theatre that privilege 'performativity' and 'a non-referential use of the body' (Li Y., 2019: 51, 54) over literariness and traditional principles of dramatic action, conflict, and mimetic representation. Rather than a genre or style, *juchang* denotes a distinctive approach to theatremaking that values contingency, situatedness, and interaction in creating a performance event. It prioritises 'the performative and spatial dimension' (Li, 2021: 165) of *chang* (site, scene) as not only a performance location but a dynamic social field, or *event-space*, generated by the 'co-presence' of performers and audience (Lehmann, 2006: 123).[3]

[3] Li's translation has sparked an intense debate on postdramatic theatre and disagreement among Chinese scholars over definitions and equivalences between drama, theatre, *xiju*, and *juchang*, with some objecting to her terminology and interpretation. For a different perspective see, for example, Gong, 2020. Most, if not all, of the artists discussed here have explicitly identified with *juchang* and commented on the resonance of Lehmann's work, as evidenced by Li's (2021) own interviews with Li Jianjun, Li Ning, Wang Mengfan, Wen Hui, and Zhao Chuan, and the conversations documented in Tuchmann, 2022. This is not to imply that all contemporary

The affirmation of *juchang* as a Chinese conjugation of the postdramatic distinguishes the ecology of postmillennial independent performance from both the logocentric canon of Chinese spoken drama (*huaju,* where *hua* means 'word') that developed in the first half of the twentieth century and the revolutionary theatre that dominated the socialist era under the respective influence of European and Soviet models of social and socialist realism. It also marks a transition from the production and organisational models that prevailed in the 1980s and 1990s, when earlier generations of postsocialist experimentalists came to the fore. From a historiographical perspective, then, while the 1980s might be described as the age of dramatists and a playwright-centred theatre, and the 1990s as the age of directors, or a director-centred theatre, the twenty-first century has emerged as the age of ensembles, marked by a constellation of independent collectives and performer-centred practices.

In the 1980s, when performing arts companies were still under the exclusive control of the state, a new cohort of experimental playwrights – including Gao Xingjian, Sha Yexin, Wang Peigong, Wei Minglun, and Zhang Xian – began to explore alternatives to both the entrenched tradition of social problem plays and psychological realism based on Ibsen and Stanislavsky, and the ideological mould of Mao-era theatrical models. A testament to the prominence of playwrights in this period is that they were more likely than directors to be the target of bans and campaigns against controversial or 'spiritually polluted' works. More radically avant-garde and postmodern aesthetics flourished in the 1990s, with the affirmation of a director's theatre epitomised by emerging figureheads such as Meng Jinghui and Mou Sen, and the veteran Lin Zhaohua. This decade also saw the formation of an embryonic independent ecology, spearheaded by new ensembles such as Mou's Garage Theatre (Xiju chejian), Tian Gebing's Paper Tiger Theatre Studio, and Wen Hui's Living Dance Studio. In retrospect, these early independent groups can be regarded as the forerunners of the postmillennial turn to *juchang*, as they paved the way for the postdramatic and performance-based approaches that distinguish twenty-first-century practice from the prevailing script- and author-centred modes of the twentieth century.

Postmillennial *juchang* artists have built on the foundations laid by the experimentalists who emerged in the premillennial phase of postsocialism. At the same time, they have further negotiated the relationship between the state and non-state sectors, working largely independently of both the socialist establishment of state-sponsored institutions and the commercial mainstream.

performance makers – even within the independent sector – have engaged with the debate or embraced these concepts, nor that the concept of *juchang* is only relevant to contemporary postdramatic performance.

They have also ventured into genres hitherto unknown or underexplored in China, including site-specific performance, physical theatre, documentary theatre, dance theatre, social and applied theatre, cyber theatre, live cinema theatre, digital performance, and cross-art formats that blur traditional boundaries between performing and visual arts practices and spaces.

Writer, curator, arts activist, and self-styled social choreographer Zhang Xian was arguably the first premillennial practitioner to articulate the postdramatic orientation of Chinese independent theatre as *hou huaju* – literally, 'post-spoken drama' (Wang and Yin, 2005: 69) – before the introduction of Lehmann's theory. More recently, Zhang has championed *juchang*, claiming that the term responds to the need for a new epistemology capable of capturing 'the germination of collective possibilities'. For Zhang, *juchang* resonates with the 'unity of life and creation' (2021: 56) pursued by artists who 'present actions' derived directly from a personal process of 'being in life' (57). *Juchang* 'is not an academic concept of art, but a way of life' (58). Zhang sees the independent artists aligned with *juchang* as a 'like-minded collective' and, essentially, an 'extended family' of 'social activists' (56) and life interventionists. Echoing this communal ethos, Li Yinan writes of '*juchang* "tribes"', which share a sense of 'togetherness' and are united in their rejection of commercialism, social divisions, and institutionalised professional hierarchies (2021: 160). The conceptual distinction between *xiju* and *juchang*, and the self-identification with either one over the other, is not merely a matter of aesthetic preference, but can also reveal a precise political choice. In practice, *juchang* is closely associated with documentary theatre (Tuchmann, 2022) and other forms of postsocialist theatre of the real, which will be explored in Section 3. However, *juchang* is inherently interdisciplinary, or even non-disciplinary, as it eschews the traditional categorisations maintained by national academies and professional industries.

Kate Elswit's reflections on the 'interconnected ecologies' of theatre and dance provide a valuable framework for considering *juchang* as 'ecosystems of practice' (2018: 20), bringing together practitioners of both theatre and dance, or rather those who do not fully identify with either, nor see their work as fitting into the traditional systems of dramatic theatre (*xiju*) and dance (*wudao*). Elswit challenges rigid distinctions between theatre and dance, emphasising instead 'entanglements' of 'expanding forms' with 'overlapping methods' (2–3). Similarly, *juchang* performances can be seen as 'expanded practices of making' (43) shared by a 'network of interlocutors' (20), breaking down conventional divisions between 'theatricality' as the domain of theatre and 'embodiment' as the domain of dance (5). In this sense, *juchang* is not only post-drama but also post-dance, or even 'postmedia' (Sarah Bay-Cheng quoted in Elswit, 2018: 69), given the prominent role of intermediality in works that conspicuously incorporate screen-based media and art installations into the embodied live material. Thus, I use 'performance' in this study precisely to highlight this expanded and entangled dimension of postmillennial independent production.

2 Performing Postsocialist Hauntologies

The first regime of temporality centres on the past and the contemporary recuperation of the revolutionary experience, also considering the resurgence of socialist values under Xi's leadership. The corresponding conceptual category refers to performance works that revisit and resignify socialist texts, genres, and iconographies to produce alternative memories and historiographies of the Mao era. I designate the performative evocation of socialist cultural legacies as *postsocialist hauntologies*.

The specific focus of this section is the politics of memory in the postsocialist afterlives of the *yangbanxi*, or 'model works' (also known as 'model operas' or 'model plays'), the dominant form of political theatre during the Cultural Revolution. I examine two productions that exhume the collective memory of this turbulent decade through ghosted practices of deconstruction and hauntological revisiting of the history of model theatre: *RED*: *A Documentary Performance* (Hong: Jilu juchang) by Wen Hui's Living Dance Studio, and *The Revolutionary Model Play 2.0* (Yangbanxi 2.0), directed by Wang Chong. The combined analysis of these productions, both premiered in 2015, reveals the hauntological qualities of postsocialist times, not only by dissecting the reanimation against the grain of the spectres of socialism – an incomplete past imperfect that continues to haunt the present – but also by illuminating contrasting approaches to remembering the past in the pre- and postmillennial cohorts of postsocialist performance makers, represented by Wen and Wang, respectively: one more subdued and conflicted, the other more inflammatory and overtly political. While Wen, born in the 1960s, belongs to a generation that personally experienced Maoism and participated in the performative reproduction of the *yangbanxi* as a child growing up during the revolution, Wang, born in the 1990s, carries only surrogate postmemories of China's radical past and has no direct experience of socialism and its performances.

2.1 Ghosting the Past (Im)Perfect: Postsocialist Afterlives of Socialist Political Theatre

Jacques Derrida begins *Specters of Marx* with a reference to Hamlet's haunting declaration upon encountering his father's ghost: 'The time is out of joint' (2006: 1). Hamlet's pronouncement suggests that hauntology, like postsocialism, is defined by temporal disjunction. Sheldon Lu's observation that 'the socialist legacy' lingers in postsocialist China 'like a ghost from a previous life' (2007: 204) resonates with Marvin Carlson's view of theatre as a potent mnemonic device, or 'memory machine', imbued with structural hauntedness and practices of '*ghosting*' (2001: 7); namely, the recasting and repetition of texts, bodies, spaces, and production elements from past theatrical manifestations. 'The present experience', Carlson writes, 'is always ghosted by previous experiences and associations while these ghosts are simultaneously shifted and modified by the processes of recycling and recollection' (2). Similarly, postsocialist performance hauntologies emerge in the critical recovery of past narratives, icons, movements, and material objects that collectively form bodies (*corpora*) of memory. Carlos Rojas highlights the hauntological quality of postsocialism – and its haunted heterochronies – when he describes China as 'shadowed by three mutually imbricated sets of apparitions: [. . .] the ghosts of capital, shades of Mao, and specters of Marx' (2016: 3–4). These spectral apparitions, corresponding to the economic realities of the neoliberal present, the institutional remnants of state socialism, and the potential for critique in the spirit of Marxism, are manifested in the postsocialist re-appropriation of socialist performance cultures, as epitomised by the contemporary culture, and culture industry, surrounding the *yangbanxi*.

A corpus of Beijing operas, dance dramas, and symphonic compositions, the *yangbanxi* were designed to model ideal representatives of the revolutionary classes of workers, peasants, and soldiers through the performative construction and reproduction of model heroes and heroines (see Pang, 2017; Ferrari, 2021). The original repertoire, canonised in 1967, consisted of eight works, with more created in the early 1970s. Jiang Qing (1914–91) oversaw the creation of these works according to strict aesthetic and ideological guidelines. A former stage and screen actress in Shanghai in the 1930s (then known as Lan Ping), Jiang married Mao in 1938 and rose to the pinnacle of radical party politics during the Cultural Revolution, gaining notoriety as the leader of the infamous Gang of Four. Following Jiang's public condemnation after Mao's death in 1976, the *yangbanxi* faded into obscurity, only to regain popularity in the 1990s amidst a broader commodification of nostalgia for socialist 'red culture'. The revival of Mao-era 'red classics' extends to tourism, advertising, television, cinema, and other popular media and industries. This contemporary remediation parallels the transmedia popularisation of the *yangbanxi* in the 1970s through films, radio broadcasts, posters, magazines, picture books, stamps, artefacts, amateur reproductions of professional versions, and adaptations in regional languages and performance genres. Official revivals have continued into the new millennium, occasionally under the patronage of Peng Liyuan, President Xi's wife and a former *yangbanxi* performer herself. Their legacy is also reflected in contemporary 'red dramas' promoting socialist themes. In 2021, *yangbanxi* were performed to celebrate the centenary of the CCP, and new stage productions created during the COVID-19 pandemic advocated exemplary behaviour in the fight against the virus and praised frontline medical workers as China's new model heroes (Wei, 2021).

Postsocialist performance hauntologies display 'an umbilical relation to the past' (Lavender, 2019: 9) that is integral to the entangled temporalities of the 'post'. This protracted, yet ambivalent, relationship emerges in equal measure from performances that both affirm and deconstruct the past. It is evident in mainstream state-sponsored dramas and in the political rituals of the CCP's 'performative state' (Ding, 2022), as well as in the independent postdramatic experiments that have flourished on the margins of performative officialdom since the millennium. Far from subscribing to Boym's 'restorative nostalgia' (2001), the works discussed in this section aim for an emancipatory recuperation of past inheritances through the production of discursive alterities. These alternatives resonate with the Derridean *revenant*, 'that which comes back' (2006: 224), manifesting as a spectral presence suspended between temporal dimensions and a hauntological force of times out of joint, conjuring up questions of justice, responsibility, and future promise (xviii–xix). The gendered herstories at the centre of both productions mobilise a performative mode of memory-making that redresses neglected memories and questions official histories. They critically intervene in the present by recalling and deconstructing the (im)perfect performances of revolutionary heroism of the socialist past.

2.2 Gendered Memoropolitics of the (Post-)Socialist Body

Gendered perspectives on the mnemonic and embodied remains of socialism are central to the '*politics* of memory, of inheritance, and of generations' (Derrida, 2006: xviii) of *RED*, choreographed by Wen Hui with a script by Zhuang Jiayun and dramaturgy by Zhuang and Kai Tuchmann.[4] Four dancers born in different decades and from different social and professional backgrounds perform a transgenerational living document that both reconstructs and deconstructs the performance archaeology and collective experience of the classic socialist ballet *The Red Detachment of Women* (Hongse niangzi jun). Created in 1964 and canonised as a *yangbanxi* in 1967, the ballet itself is a remediation, or revolutionary upgrading, of Xie Jin's 1961 film of the same title, based on historical accounts of an all-female army unit active on Hainan Island in the 1930s and earlier textual and theatrical adaptations. The film version of the model ballet was released in 1970. *RED* approaches these

[4] For a video excerpt, see Wen Hui and Living Dance Studio (2018).

canonical texts through gendered corporeal memory, in line with Wen's belief that 'female memory begins with the body':

> Memory is the body's mark of experience. [. . .] Through our work as dancers, we explore how the body records not only individual histories, but those involving change in the greater social arena as well. [. . .] In the end, the body is that threshold we must cross in pursuit of the memories within. (2013: 133–34)

Dance scholar Chiayi Seetoo has examined Wen's 'dramaturgy of the corporeal' (2021) in the context of her long-standing choreographic work with the Living Dance Studio, the independent company she co-founded in 1994 with documentary filmmaker Wu Wenguang. Film scholar Zhang Zhen has highlighted the 'search of a women-centered expressive dimension as both a bodily archive and an intimate-public sphere' in Wen's performative first-person documentaries (2020: 2). Writing about *RED*, Zhuang Jiayun describes a comparable creative process that harnesses 'the body as a research method' (2017) to uncover personal and collective testimonies. According to Zhuang, *RED* positions the body as an instrument for phenomenological cognition and biopolitical critique of the ideological inscription of bodies and of the discipline imposed on them in revolutionary mass culture, as epitomised by the *yangbanxi* project. As outlined in the synopsis produced for the international tour, *RED* seeks to 'anatomize' the past through the body's roles as 'an archive', 'witness and carrier of history', 'catalyst for memory', and 'site of transgressive impulses' – thereby also contributing to the gendered, genealogical construction of critical counter-memories.[5]

The stage performance blends choreographic movement and oral narration with screen media elements. These include footage from the 1961 and 1970 *Red Detachment* films, performance stills, images of blocking diagrams of the original choreography and character illustrations from a production manual of the model ballet, and video interviews conducted by Wen, Zhuang, and Zou Xueping (not seen on video) with witnesses and participants in the creation and dissemination of *yangbanxi* culture in the 1970s. The interviewees are the theatremaker and arts activist Zhang Xian, two Chinese scholars based in Beijing and the United States, a Chinese NGO worker, and three retired professional dancers from municipal and provincial-level companies in Yunnan, Wen's home region. Here, Wen first encountered the *yangbanxi* as a child, learning the moves from films and photographs. One of these dancers, Liu Zhuying, also participates in the live performance alongside Wen, Jiang Fan, and Li Xinmin. The other two, Wang Huifen and Zhang Laishan, former interpreters of the ballet's female and male

[5] This text appears in the programmes produced for the BOK Festival in Macau (2016) and Dance Umbrella in London (2018). Part of the analysis of *RED* draws on Ferrari (2021).

protagonists Wu Qinghua and Hong Changqing, are featured in the video interviews. In the closing scenes, Zhang Laishan is shown onscreen teaching dance steps to schoolchildren, accompanied by music from the model ballet.

RED comprises three acts. The first act, titled 'Marching Forward' ('Xiang qian jin') after the theme song of *Red Detachment*, traces the genealogy of the model ballet. Wen discusses the ideological principles behind the creation of the *yangbanxi*. Photographs of the older dancers in their revolutionary stage roles appear onscreen, interspersed with recollections of the ballet from the dancers on stage and the video interviewees. In this and the next act, 'Getting Intertwined', the dancers demonstrate parts of the original choreography, supported by on-screen images from the production manual (Figure 1). Footage from the 1961 film is also shown and discussed. Intimate memories of performing, watching, and experiencing *Red Detachment* are shared both on stage and on screen, progressively diverging from the official discourse surrounding its creation and heritage. The third act, 'Looking Back', explores the complexities of remembering and forgetting the revolutionary experience, the ambivalent feelings of nostalgia and discomfort tied to the postsocialist resurgence of the model ballet, its enduring influence on contemporary performance cultures, and its potential future legacies. *RED* revisits the life of *Red Detachment* at the levels of both state policy and daily practice. However, by deconstructing the ontology of the official model, the production effectively

Figure 1 *RED: A Documentary Performance* (2015). Image courtesy of Wen Hui/Living Dance Studio (Photographer: Ricky Wong)

performs its hauntology, uncovering its posthumous afterlife and highlighting ordinary experiences of socialism through the real-life testimonies and private memories of successive generations of dancers and audiences.

Each of the four dancers is associated with a unique movement that reflects a distinctive typology of somatic, affective, and material memory. Born in 1955 and 1960 respectively, Liu and Wen grew up in the socialist system and experienced the revolution and the culture of the *yangbanxi* first-hand. Liu took on various roles in *Red Detachment* during the 1970s. At the time of her involvement in *RED*, she was coordinating amateur groups of *guangchang wu*, or 'dancing in public spaces', a popular community activity practised mainly, though not exclusively, by middle-aged women and associated with the collectivist culture of the Mao era (Seetoo and Zou, 2016). Wen graduated from the Beijing Dance Academy and choreographed for a state company before training in modern dance in the United States and Europe. She eventually broke away from both academic dance and the state system to form her own ensemble, advocating for equality and individuality and rejecting codified roles and fixed rules, in contrast to the rigid prescriptions of the *yangbanxi*. As Zhuang observes, Liu and Wen respectively embody a revolutionary body that adheres to the model and a conflictual body that resists the biopolitical standardisation enforced 'by revolution and labor' (2017). Wen's movements convey both discomfort and emotional ambiguity towards the socialist past, which has shaped both her personal trajectory as a dancer and the broader cultural discourse of postsocialism. Many interviewees on screen similarly express ambivalent feelings of nostalgia laced with unease about the collective legacies of the revolution. Wen's bodily archive also acts as a bridge between generations of dancing bodies: the socialist bodies of Liu, Wang, and Zhang, and the postsocialist bodies of Jiang and Li, both born in 1988. Her body straddles the interlocking temporal regimes of two eras and the mnemonic regimes of two generations, connecting the direct memory of the former with the prosthetic memory of the latter – namely, an indirect and mediated knowledge of the revolution and its theatrical inheritances.

Jiang, a professional dancer, demonstrates complex choreographic diagrams from the model ballet's manual, displayed on the screen. Jiang's is a trained body trying to break free from the constraints of academic dance and unleash a 'natural body', as Zhuang (2017) describes her performance. Li, a rural-to-urban migrant and the only nonprofessional dancer in the production, also signifies a natural, spontaneous body and a somatic memory shaped neither by revolution nor dance training, but by the rigours of manual labour and a challenging childhood. *RED* intertwines the narrative of *Red Detachment*'s female protagonist, who leaves a life of oppression for a brighter future in the revolutionary women's army, with Li's personal journey from marginalised worker to independent artist. After migrating to Beijing from an impoverished region, Li worked as a caretaker at the CCD Workstation and later became involved in Wen and Wu's film and performance projects. The lived experience of her labouring body is repeatedly juxtaposed with elements of the ballet in ways that disrupt the aestheticised heroic representations of the model scenario. In one scene, Li recalls a photograph from the ballet manual that triggers memories of being humiliated by a teacher and eventually dropping out of school due to her parents' inability to afford tuition fees. The photograph depicts the CCP representative and army commander, Hong Changqing, lecturing the women soldiers in front of a blackboard. In another instance, Liu discusses a broadsword prop from the ballet. This reminds Li of a sword her blacksmith father crafted for chopping wood, and the hard manual labour she performed as a child, cutting trees in the mountains. This prop also brings to mind another farming tool – a knife her father made for slaughtering pigs, which her mother kept at her bedside for protection after his untimely death.

Finally, the production features the mediated bodies of the video interviewees and those of the original *yangbanxi* performers shown in projected footage. A spectral aesthetic configuration takes shape, as the immaterial silhouettes of the model heroes and heroines appear on the screen alongside the tangible bodies of the dancers on stage. The mnemonic repository of living, moving bodies and mediated images from the postsocialist present retains the ephemeral traces of past cultural formations that persist in popular leisure activities such as *guangchang wu*, mainstream productions, and official revivals.[6] While demonstrating a choreographic treatment from the ballet in the final act, Wen reflects: 'I wonder if this has become a legacy that will pass effortlessly from one generation to the next' (Wen Hui and Living Dance Studio, 2022: 173).

In an interesting twist, the *Red Detachment* theme song has found new life as a feminist anthem in postsocialist China. Women's rights activists fighting institutional abuse and corruption in Hainan have adopted the song, as documented by Wang Nanfu in the film *Hooligan Sparrow* (2016), and so have factory workers protesting in Shenzhen. These performative and sometimes improvised revivals, which creep into the present like uninvited spectral appearances, are all manifestations of postsocialist performance hauntologies. They redress the socialist past through re-signification and 'memory activism as the *strategic commemoration of a contested past to achieve mnemonic or political change by working outside state channels*' (Gutman and Wüstenberg, 2023: 5). Like *RED*, these actions imbue contemporary remains of that past with

[6] The National Ballet of China (Zhongyang balei wutuan) revived *Red Detachment* in 1992 and has performed it widely in China and abroad, not without controversy.

alternative meanings. They also underline a crucial connection between the operations of postsocialist hauntologies and questions of justice and accountability for past traumas and present inequalities; for, as Derrida asserts, '[i]f I am getting ready to speak at length about ghosts, inheritance, and generations, [. . .] it is in the name of *justice*' (2006: xviii).

RED explores various facets of the hauntological revisiting of socialist redness: red culture, red memory, red heroism, and the 'five red categories' (*hong wu lei*) of peasants, workers, revolutionary soldiers, cadres, and martyrs. At one point, Wen discusses the positive and negative characters of *Red Detachment* over an illustration from the manual, explaining the principle of the 'three prominences' (*san tuchu*). This principle emphasises the positive characters, among them the heroic characters, and among these, the main hero or heroine. But there are also the red of the blood on the dancers' aching feet from performing the model ballets on a threshing ground, and the dirt of the soft mud on their ballet shoes, as Liu and Wang recall in their interviews; and the blood and dirt of hard labour, as Li's stories reveal, and those of maternal bodies and sexual desire. All these different shades of red seep from the dancers' somatic archives to reveal an alternative view to the official memory of the immaculate, sublime, almost superhuman, and supposedly desexualised physiques of the model characters, and of those who embodied them. These are energetic and enthusiastic bodies, but also exhausted, conflicted, longing, imperfect, and ultimately real.

The organic materiality of flesh and blood bodies is perhaps most revealing in Wang's account of her return to the stage after childbirth in 1972. In her embodied mnemonic archive, the connection between body and labour concerns not the body forged by manual labour, as in Li's case, but by reproductive labour. The former ballerina was told to take an injection to stop her breast milk production so that she could continue performing. During one rehearsal, the milk intended for the newborn started dripping onto the floor, mixed with sweat from her skin, and eventually stopped naturally after three days of gruelling training, due to exhaustion. In other scenes, the male interviewees recall how young men were secretly aroused by the titillating images of the model dancers' perfect bodies in tight military uniforms. Their accounts resonate with the experience of a generation socialised in the culture of revolutionary puritanism of the Mao era. Like the dancers' stories of blood, dirt, and physical exertion, these narratives deconstruct the master discourse surrounding the *yangbanxi* and the collectivist culture of the masses of that era. Overall, *RED* offers a significant articulation of postsocialist performance hauntologies, exposing not only the blind spots and contradictions of socialism, but also its lingering affective and social resonance, like a ghost that won't go away.

2.3 Socialist Histories 2.0: Remediating Madame Mao

The unsettled ghosts of socialism resurface in *The Revolutionary Model Play 2.0* (hereafter *Model Play*). Combining live performance and video feeds, historical film footage, and a documentary script based on biographical writings and archival materials, Wang Chong's production revisits the controversial legacy of Jiang Qing, the ideological architect of the *yangbanxi*. It presents both a spectral resurrection of Jiang's public and private history and a mediated dissection of the political and aesthetic genealogy of model theatre.

Model Play is part of a '2.0' series of intermedial adaptations that Wang's company, Théâtre du Rêve Expérimental, inaugurated in 2012 with the 'stage cinema' (*wutai dianying*) production *Thunderstorm 2.0* (Leiyu 2.0), a deconstructive treatment of Cao Yu's classic realist drama (1934). This was followed by *The Warfare of Landmine 2.0* (Dilei zhan 2.0, premiered in 2013), based on the 1962 socialist film of the same title, *Ghosts 2.0* (Qungui 2.0, premiered in 2014), after Ibsen, and others. The designation of each piece as a 2.0 upgrade of an existing text underscores the prominent role of digital technology in their production and staging, particularly the integration of on-site filming, editing, and screening into the live performance. *Model Play* is no exception, as the action on stage is mediated by ubiquitous video cameras and live video feeds. Here, however, the titular 2.0 foregrounds not only strategies of postdramatic versioning, but also the reiteration of socialist histories and iconographies, hence the workings of '[t]he medium of performance [as] a technology of remembrance' (Bleeker, 2012: 2). The process of media updating doubles as a hauntological medium, enabling both a spectropoetic return of the socialist past to the postsocialist present and a spectropolitical remediation of a suppressed historical record. The concept of remediation in *Model Play* carries multiple connotations. Formally, the past is *remediated* through the extensive use of the filmic medium to reconstruct Jiang's biography and the history of the *yangbanxi* under her leadership. But the past is also *remedied*, according to an alternative etymology of remediation as an act of repair, restoration, and rectification of something that is defective and undesirable, or that has been distorted and inadequately processed – as is the case with the official record surrounding Madame Mao as a ghosted political figure in the PRC.

Jiang left a complex legacy after Mao's death and her arrest in 1976. Vilified as the ringleader of the Gang of Four and caricatured as a monstrous 'white-boned demon', she became a focal point of blame for the radicalism of the Cultural Revolution. Despite her fierce defence during the televised show trials of 1980–81 that she was nothing more than 'Chairman Mao's dog', she was made a scapegoat for the brutality of a tumultuous decade and sentenced to death, later commuted to life imprisonment. Her suicide in 1991 was barely and belatedly reported in the official media, and her political history was written off as the history of degeneration of a power-hungry woman who ruthlessly persecuted private and public enemies in a quest for personal revenge. Branded as a conspirator and a counterrevolutionary renegade, she was effectively erased from official discourse. As Tani Barlow writes in an essay on the historiographical necessity of 'taking Jiang Qing seriously': 'Jiang Qing was everywhere. One of four parts of the Gang of Four and a crucial member of the leadership, yet she has been made inessential historiographically. It is hard to think of another name so systemically power dwarfed and approached more anxiously as Jiang' (2017: 1). By attempting to reassess this history, *Model Play* resonates with the Derridean intimation of speaking to the ghost in order to do justice. This does not imply an exoneration of Jiang's responsibility or a reversal of her historical judgement. Rather, through a mix of documentary and fictional re-enactments of key political and performance moments from the period of Jiang's political rise, the production expands the scope for reviewing this history from multiple angles, revealing contrasting refractions of both her public and private personas, and restoring her presence in a protracted historiography of absence. In this sense, the project responds to Barlow's invitation to take Jiang Qing seriously.

Model Play both reconstructs and deconstructs the historical record. It documents in unflinching detail the violence Jiang unleashed, the abuse she mandated, and how she used her position to pursue personal vendettas and inflict untold suffering on those she felt had wronged her. Yet, by integrating testimonies from historical actors of the era – supporters, detractors, victims, and witnesses – with Jiang's own account, the production overwrites the unambiguously damning leitmotif entrenched in official history with a polyphony of contrasting voices. This approach fosters the emergence of alternative narratives and prompts new questions about a person and a period still shrouded in secrecy. The dominant discourse cast a woman with 'empress' ambitions as the arch villain in a grand revolutionary act, but one that she could not have performed alone: not without her consort's support as the backstage director of a national political drama, nor without the active participation of a radicalised mass in a collective witch-hunt that left no one untouched. As the performance text suggests: 'Jiang Qing was mad, but who wasn't at the time? Yet we gave all the credits to her, blaming her as the sole dancer with the devil.'[7]

It is no coincidence that Zhao Binghao, a Chinese playwright then living in the United States, based his script on American historian Roxane Witke's

[7] This and subsequent quotations are from the English version of the script provided by Wang Chong, written by Zhao Binghao, and translated by Tian Hongyi. For a video excerpt, see Théâtre du Rêve Expérimental (2015).

Comrade Chiang Ch'ing (1977). Witke's was the first biography of Jiang and the only one written from the biographer's direct interactions with her subject, and thus the closest we have to Jiang's own account, in the absence of an autobiography.[8] Nor is it surprising that the production, with its head-on confrontation of Jiang's historical spectre and its explicit critique of revolutionary excess, was not staged in China (or elsewhere) after its premiere at the Singapore International Festival of Arts, where Wang directed a multiethnic and multilingual cast from the LASALLE College of the Arts.

Unlike other works in the 2.0 series, *Model Play* is neither an updated version nor an intermedial adaptation of a specific *yangbanxi*. Projected footage of several model plays punctuates the performance, and many of the artists who contributed to their creation appear as characters, documenting their history and legacy. At the heart of the production, however, is the parable of Jiang's rise and fall as a revolutionary model drama itself, as it played out on the historical stage of late Maoism. On this public stage, the private woman – the former actress and leader's wife – lived out the political model of the revolutionary heroine. After the curtain fell on the revolution, she was recast as a model villain. Paradoxically, official history reproduced the moral polarities inscribed in the aesthetic prescriptions of the dramas that the heroine-turned-villain herself had orchestrated. Jiang's life was a *yangbanxi*, and its 2.0 upgrade presents a multi-voiced reassessment of her revolutionary performance.

Model Play is both a reflection on the limits of historiographical writing and a performative biography of the historiographical subject. Witke's rather benign portrayal could itself be read as a performative biography. During the days the two women spent together in 1972, Jiang played to Witke the person she wanted the world to know, and Witke chose to tell '[h]er personal history largely as she presented it' (1977: 445). *Model Play* is also a dissection of Jiang's personal past and her place in the revolution, as she herself suggested to Witke: 'Let me dissect myself before you' (5). But Wang's deconstructive remediation of Madame Mao's biography subjects the notion of performativity to a 2.0-style doubling process. This occurs not only because Jiang and Witke appear as characters in a script (Zhao's) based on Witke's book, as performers of the performative biography, but also through the metatheatrical device of inserting the fictional playwright Yu Zhongkai into the script. Struggling with a commission to write a play about Jiang, Yu seeks Witke's advice and engages the historian in an extended debate about Madame Mao's multiple identities, the cultural significance of the *yangbanxi*, and the relationship between people and power, which is essentially about the irreducibility of historiographical truth.

[8] On Jiang's biographies, see Salino (2021).

Yu and Witke's narratives are complemented by accounts from historical figures who knew her as the glamorous actress Lan Ping, the revolutionary leader Jiang Qing, or both. These include old acquaintances from her stage and screen heyday in Shanghai, including her former husband, the left-wing critic Tang Na (1914–88); the filmmaker Zheng Junli (1911–69), who died in custody three years after his house was ransacked, allegedly on Jiang's orders, during the Cultural Revolution; and his wife, the actress Huang Chen (1914–94), who testified at her trial. Artists involved in the creation of the *yangbanxi* also appear: Composer and Minister of Culture Yu Huiyong (1925–77), who killed himself after being arrested for conspiring with the Gang of Four; Beijing opera actor Qian Haoliang (1934–2020), who starred in *The Red Lantern* (Hong deng ji); director and playwright A Jia (1907–94), who co-wrote and directed the play; dancer Liu Qingtang (1932–2010), star of *Red Detachment* and later Vice-Minister of Culture, known as a sexual predator and serial informer who drove many artists to political persecution and suicide; and his co-star, ballerina Bai Shuxiang (1939–), who was sentenced to hard labour after Liu abused and denounced her. Gang of Four member Zhang Chunqiao (1917–2005) is portrayed as an uncanny baby-doll-like puppet, reflecting Yu Zhongkai's cynical view of the revolution as 'only politicians and fools and puppets and a play'.

The media design of *Model Play* supports the production's intention to undertake a biographical dissection of its subject in order to facilitate a multi-perspective examination of the possibility of historical truth. Four static cameras capture the characters' personal memories and experiences of working with (or against) Jiang. These live feeds are displayed on a large screen made of tea-stained Cultural Revolution-era newspapers (Figure 2). The screen periodically

Figure 2 *The Revolutionary Model Play 2.0* (2015), directed by Wang Chong. Image courtesy of Théâtre du Rêve Expérimental.

splits into four sections, as the actors speak to the cameras simultaneously. This configuration alternates with the use of a handheld camera, operated by Yu and Witke in turn, and then four cameras wielded by armed policemen in a scene restaging the arrest of Yu Huiyong, Qian Haoliang, Liu Qingtang, and Zhang Chunqiao as members of the 'Jiang Qing Counterrevolutionary Group'. While the dialogue is in English, the actors deliver their monologues and confide their characters' most intimate thoughts to the camera in their native languages (French, Tamil, Malay, Mandarin, German, Tagalog, and Korean). The linguistic shift allows both psychological identification for the actors and emotional distance for the audience, for example when Witke breaks into Tamil and Jiang pours out her childhood memories in Korean. As narratives overlap and images are relayed in real time, the camera assumes the dual role of historical witness and confessional device. The performance thus renders a multi-experiential testimony, in which Jiang's voice is restored to the record against a normative historiography of silence and erasure. However, the fragmented screen and the subjective lens of the handheld camera, interchangeably positioned as both perpetrator and victim, constantly remind the audience that this voice is only one in a dissonant chorus of competing utterances. And so, the ultimate question of historical responsibility remains unanswered. Yet, as Witke declares in a rare moment when the speaking subject is not mediated by cameras and screens: 'Questions are more important than answers.'

Projected footage of the *yangbanxi* on screen intersperses grotesque scenes of escalating brutality on stage, spectacularly enhanced by the routine explosion of water bombs filled with blood-red liquid and a relentless deluge of pouring rain. The contrast between mediated and live performance in turn magnifies the discrepancy between the polished, media-induced façade of socialist utopia that the model plays fabricated for the public and the dystopian scenarios played out in the private lives of their creators. Unlike the reflective nostalgia occasionally present in *RED*, *Model Play* conveys the aversive structure of feeling towards the past that Martin Baake-Hansen calls nostophobia: 'Nostalgia cleans up the past, while nostophobia displays its dirt' (2015: 122). *Model Play* echoes and amplifies the blood, sweat, and dirt on the bodies and feet of the dancers in *RED* – as signifiers of the emotional and physical labour of the revolution – with copious bloody water from the bursting bombs, the blood-stained propaganda newspapers, and the hour-long torrential rain, which slowly mixes with the red liquids splattered on the floor and cascades back onto the stage in a bloody downpour. In a climactic scene, aptly titled 'Blood and Dirt', the water obstructs the actors and obscures the camera lenses as the dirt of the revolution finally rears its ugly head. Their movements on the slippery, flooded stage become precarious and their bodies drenched and dirty – as dirty as the political machinations taking place behind the scenes, and as precarious as their personal standing – as the overwhelming tide of the revolution rises and finally collapses, with an angry crowd rushing to the scene and tearing the newspaper screen to shreds.

Model Play's intermedial strategies reveal an additional mode of remediation as the re-enactment of collective memory, by reconfiguring the mnemonic inheritance of socialism and socialist drama within a postdramatic framework of 'postsocialist postmemory' (Li, 2020: 214). In line with Marianne Hirsch's canonical definition of postmemory, this remediated past speaks to 'the relationship that the "generation after" bears to the personal, collective, and cultural trauma of those who came before – to experiences they "remember" only by means of the stories, images, and behaviors among which they grew up' (2012: 5). The spiralling cycle of mutual accusation, exoneration, denial, and self-defence that the production entrusts to the media apparatus, and the fragmented archive that it assembles, bring into focus both a vision of history as constructed of multiple subjective truths, and the elusiveness of a conclusive verdict on the biographical subject's place in that history. Faced with the undecidability of history and the difficulty of doing justice to the spectres of the past, the post-generation resorts to hauntological strategies of resuscitation and redress, 'mediated not by recall but by imaginative investment, projection, and creation' (5) – in other words, strategies of storytelling. Wang drove this point home in a public lecture entitled 'Is Madame Mao Dead?' held online at the University of Vienna on 7 April 2021. The director concluded his reflection on the play and its historical significance with a quote from the opening monologue of the HBO miniseries *Chernobyl* (2019), which also provides a fitting conclusion to this analysis:

> What is the cost of lies? [. . .] It's not that we'll mistake them for the truth. The real danger is that if we hear *enough* lies, then we no longer recognize the truth at all. What can we do then? What else is left but to abandon even the hope of truth, and content ourselves instead . . . with *stories*. [. . .] In these stories, it doesn't matter who the heroes are. All we want to know is: who is to blame? (Mazin, 2018: 1)

3 Performing Postsocialist Realisms

The second regime of temporality focuses on the present and the corresponding conceptual category of *postsocialist realisms*. This modality of performances of postsocialist times encompasses a variety of practices that foreground subaltern communities and ordinary citizens as embodied archives, texts, and documents, bearing witness to narratives of resistance and survival, current social conditions, private micro-histories, and the mundane routines of everyday life. It includes works that register the postsocialist experience as it unfolds in the fluid zone of the present continuous tense, striving to capture the contingency and complexity of a fragmented reality in constant flux.

These performances in the present continuous align with global descriptions of reality-based theatre and dance that unsettle, or even renounce, immanent notions of truth, authenticity, and representational totality by embracing non-mimetic approaches to the real. Elsewhere, I have categorised these practices as 'postsocialist theatre of the real' (Ferrari, 2023), drawing on definitions of 'theatre of the real' (Martin, 2013) and 'theatre of real people' (Garde and Mumford, 2016) from theatre studies, and concepts from the scholarship of Chinese art and cinema. Rather than close readings, this section offers an overview of a wider range of works in order to identify significant points of convergence between postsocialist performances of the real and theorisations of postsocialist film and visual culture; namely, a conceptual resonance with the notion of postsocialist realism; an embodied documentary approach based on principles of liveness, immediacy, and *xianchang*; a poetics of ordinariness; and an aesthetics of ruin.

3.1 Postsocialist Theatre of the Real: Recording Reality in the Present Continuous

Jason McGrath introduces the term 'postsocialist realism' to describe post-Maoist filmmaking practices that depart from the 'prescriptive realism' of socialist cinema by incorporating neorealist and documentary aesthetics. These films also move away from the formulaic tendencies of the state-sponsored 'main melody' (*zhuxuanlü*) genre that replaced revolutionary realism during the reform era. McGrath suggests that this late twentieth-century 'post-*socialist realism*' has evolved into 'postsocialist *realism*' in the globalised twenty-first century. The postmillennial realist mode remains committed to documenting contemporary realities, while distancing itself from the latest prescriptive trends of neopropaganda blockbusters and commercial '*capitalist* realism' that fuel the CCP's neoliberal dream (2022: 275–76).

A similar claim can be made for postmillennial *juchang* practices that reject normative dramaturgies, consumerist entertainment spectacles, and official neo-model theatre. Zhao Chuan, the founder of Grass Stage and a prominent advocate of social theatre in China, reflects a widespread sentiment among independent practitioners when he states: 'I think in the very beginning, the reason I made theatre was due to dissatisfaction. There was a lack of reality, a deficiency of truth where I lived. [. . .] So for me, the theatre became a way to the real' (2022: 60). The modes of *documentary* and *embodied* realism that characterise the postsocialist theatre of the real (Ferrari, 2023) challenge the conservative canon of mimetic realism and the (melo)dramatic excess typical of the performance and production styles that dominate the institutional and commercial mainstream. Instead, they aim to present a lived reality dynamically and often precariously caught up in the whirlwind of postsocialist transformation, drawing on archives and bodies situated in the present moment.

As a performative articulation of postsocialist realism, the postsocialist theatre of the real also testifies to the convergence of postdramatic *juchang*, as a key descriptor of independent postsocialist performance, and *xianchang*, as the founding principle of a new mode of site-specific or 'on-the-spot' realism (Berry, 2009) in independent cinema since the 1990s. Documentary filmmaker Wu Wenguang anchors *xianchang* in the temporality of the present by suggesting that the term denotes 'the present tense' (*xianzai shi*) and (being present) 'on the scene' (*zai chang*) (2000: 274) – namely, presence on location in the present moment (see also Robinson, 2013: 29–32). Both *juchang* and *xianchang* prioritise the embodied situatedness of a (filmic, performance) event or action in the specific *event-space* of the *chang* (site, scene, location) and the immediacy of documenting such a live event or action as it unfolds in the contingent temporal dimension of the present continuous.

In this framework, reality is not 'staged' or aesthetically reconstituted, but observed and recorded, and experienced and expressed through the body. Reality is neither beautified nor sanitised, neither homogeneous nor harmonious (or 'harmonised' – a popular Chinese euphemism for 'censored'), but revealed in all its raw contradictions. Performances of postsocialist realism challenge conventional notions of the theatrical real embedded in mimesis and reproducibility by embracing a documentary disposition mixed with embodied performativity. There is no representation, but rather present-*ation* as a process of doing, of actualising reality – an action of real-*isation* that takes place in the continuous real time of the present. Director Li Jianjun, founder of the New Youth Group in Beijing in 2011, echoes the postdramatic critique of theatre based on reproduction (*zaixian*) and the ontological totality of artistic representation. He expresses scepticism about the constructed theatricality of 'reproducible theatre' (2019: 210) and argues for a perception of reality as an agentive process of 'becoming' (real) rather than an immanent state of being (real) (212).

Li Ning, a performance artist and filmmaker who founded the Physical Guerrillas in 1997 in Jinan, Shandong, explains that his work 'reconstructs reality' (*chonggou xianshi*) (Li, 2021: 128) and is based on 'presentation' (*chengxian*) rather than 'representation' (*biaoxian*) (Li, 2018: 59). His physical theatre (*zhiti juchang*) is grounded in 'body sketching' (*zhiti xiesheng*), a concept derived from life sketching in the visual arts that emphasises the observation and description of the physical (tactile, auditory, kinetic) properties of objects and materials through the medium of the body. Body sketching leads to a second stage of 'body regeneration' (*zhiti zaisheng*), in which bodies adopt the attributes of these objects and materials to develop fragments of movement that are later assembled into a cohesive performance presentation (60–62). Li's first-person documentary *Tape* (Jiaodai, 2010) captures this creative process. *Tape* is also the title of a 2007 performance recorded in the film, in which the artist and his company of mostly nonprofessional performers test the material and abstract qualities of adhesive tape with their bodies to create dance sequences and sound effects. These qualities – stickiness, resilience, randomness, flexibility, cohesion – are then invested with broader meanings that reflect personal experiences, social interactions, and the many incidental situations they encounter during the guerrilla execution of the project, as the ensemble struggles to survive amidst the vagaries of a ruthless reality.[9]

The extensive corpus of postmillennial performances of postsocialist realism can be grouped into two broad clusters, each characterised by distinctive thematic orientations, dramaturgical strategies, and political agendas, which I subsume as *dramaturgies of precarity* and *dramaturgies of the quotidian.*

Dramaturgies of precarity encompass projects that draw attention to underrepresented experiences of economic inequality and civic marginalisation affecting subaltern (*diceng*; literally, 'low stratum') social groups. These disenfranchised communities are often neglected or negatively profiled in public discourse and mainstream media. Cross-societal alliances between artists, intellectuals, labour organisations, and NGOs led to a growth in community and social theatre initiatives in the period leading up to President Xi's inauguration in 2013 and the nationwide crackdown on social movements that intensified after 2015. These activist networks have reclaimed space, voice, and agency for the vast urban precariat, made up largely of rural migrants employed in the construction and service industries of China's sprawling megalopolises. They have also exposed the dehumanising living (and dying) conditions of factory workers on the assembly lines of the Pearl River Delta. Notable in this context are Grass Stage's touring productions of *Little Society* (Xiao shehui, 2009–11) and *World Factory* (Shijie gongchang, 2014–16). Both works demonstrate a commitment to raising awareness of the plight of what Margaret Hillenbrand describes as a 'de facto underclass' consigned to a state of exception and systemic exclusion, which she terms 'zombie citizenship' (2023: 2–3).

The cast of *World Factory* included singer-songwriter Xu Duo, co-founder of the NGO Migrant Workers Home (Gongyou zhi jia) and a member of the New

[9] Excerpts from the film and performance versions of *Tape*, as well as videos of other Physical Guerrillas productions discussed in this section, are available on the Théâtre Sens YouTube channel (@theatresens5122).

Workers Art Troupe (Xin gongren yishu tuan), based in the migrant village of Picun on the outskirts of Beijing. Since its founding in 2002, this worker-artist ensemble has initiated numerous performance projects of its own. Grass Stage also worked with labour organisations in Shenzhen – home to electronics manufacturer Foxconn – to develop *World Factory*, a collective creation (Connery, 2020). Grass Stage's collaboration with Foxconn workers and activists led to the establishment of the North Gate Theatre Troupe (Beimen jushe) in Shenzhen in 2016, with the support of the local NGO Qinghu Xuetang. Factory workers devised and performed real-life situations in the collective creations *Our Stories* (Women de gushi), a series launched in 2016, and *The Xiao Ping Incident* (Xiao Ping shijian, produced in 2017–19), which documented labour disputes involving women workers. However, both the troupe and the NGO were forced to cease operations in 2019 due to escalating repression of grassroots activism (Jaguścik, 2022). The testimonies of the postsocialist precariat that animate these projects echo Hillenbrand's astute diagnosis of 'precarity as a master term for the present' (2023: 3) and postsocialism's 'core partner term', noting that '[p]recarity and postsocialism are twin conditions' (26) in postmillennial China.

Dramaturgies of the quotidian instead refer to performances that share a similar documentary or ethnographic approach to the real, but seek to articulate a poetics of the mundane and the ordinary that elevates the lived experience of 'the nameless mankind' to artistic form. Li Jianjun coined the term to describe a kind of theatre that takes everyday reality and the bodies, voices, and histories of subjects from all walks of life as its raw material. As he writes: 'The nameless mankind' (*wuming de ren*) 'are people standing on the ruins of temples, everyday people, people in the plural, hidden people, broken people, fabricated people, blurred people, people waiting to be named' (2019: 212). Dramaturgies of the quotidian include the New Youth Group's documentary theatre with nonprofessional performers; Wang Mengfan's dance theatre with middle-aged women, children, and retired ballet dancers, which celebrates ordinary bodies in motion; and the performances of the Physical Guerrillas, in which untrained or imperfect bodies interact with prosaic materials. These artists of the quotidian explore narratives of ordinary living and the agency of common bodies in daily life situations, valorising practices of 'deskilling' and 'pedestrian vocabularies to find new connections between art and life' (Elswit, 2018: 45). While there is a fairly substantial body of scholarship on performances of precarity, particularly in relation to Grass Stage and the Picun community, these more recent approaches to the quotidian have not yet been extensively studied, despite their growing prominence in the postmillennial *juchang* landscape. This underexplored area will therefore be the focus of the next section.

3.2 Documenting Ordinary People, Dancing Real Bodies

The poetics of ordinariness that informs the New Youth Group's approach to the realities of the postsocialist present operates on multiple levels in their practice of *fanren juchang* – a term coined by Li Jianjun that I have translated as 'theatre of the ordinary' (Ferrari, 2023). A more direct rendering might be 'theatre of real people' (Garde and Mumford, 2016), in line with Wang Mengfan's English description of her practice of *fanren wudao juchang* as 'dance theatre of real people'. Both concepts are rooted in dramaturgies of the quotidian that foreground ordinary situations, narratives, and bodies, and seek to capture the emotional experiences and physical expressions of common people.

The New Youth Group's *A Man Who Flies Up to the Sky* (Fei xiang tiankong de ren), premiered in 2015, presents a contemplative visual document of domestic urban life in China. Set in a wooden box resembling a rundown domestic interior, the performance unfolds through a series of semi-static tableaux based on the repetitive depiction of prosaic routines and ordinary life situations. Eight performers silently embody over thirty characters of different ages and identities, changing masks and costumes in over forty snapshots of life. The scenes, each lasting only a few minutes, range from people eating, resting, smoking, and cleaning to posing for family portraits, fiddling with mobile phones, playing cards, fighting, ageing, and simply living. The repetitive accumulation of everyday rituals aims to provide a choral testimony to the anxieties of modernisation in a rapidly changing social environment. While these condensed snippets of nameless humanity are mute, succeeding one another in slow motion like frames from a silent film, each individual image is followed by a matching soundscape of field recordings, voiceovers, music, and assorted noises. The sound delay and the resulting asynchrony between the visual and the auditory elements within each scene reflect the dissonant structure of feeling of the postsocialist present. The temporal structure – punctuated by 'thematic repetition' within a slow-paced sequence of interchangeable fragments and 'non-reproducible actions' (Li J., 2019: 214) – constructs an impressionistic display of still life that not only registers the weariness and monotony of ordinary existence, but also conveys a sense of mundane intimacy, inviting the discovery of subtle meanings in the ordinary. Li argues for a calculated randomness within repetition as a crucial aesthetic principle in the revelation of the real that results from the collision of action and stillness in this production: 'The repetitive structure fits my perception of the essence of the everyday and of the extraordinary' (214).

The so-called Amateur Trilogy (Suren sanbuqu) is an emblematic embodiment of the theatre of the ordinary. The series invites nonprofessional performers from diverse backgrounds to share personal narratives as collective creators and storytellers. Private memories, experiences, and aspirations provide the dramaturgical material, and ordinary people performing real-life stories become the performance text. For the original production of *One Fine Day* (Meihao de yi tian), premiered in 2013, nineteen participants of different ages, professions, and social identities were recruited in Beijing through casting calls, workshops, and interviews. During the performance, they deliver simultaneous monologues sitting in a row of chairs at the front of the stage. Each wears a microphone connected to a unique radio frequency marked on the floor (Figure 3). The audience can tune into the different individual channels with receivers and listen to an extended compilation of auditory life fragments through headsets. Timed explosions of firecrackers and the whistling of amplified kettles placed on a stove

Figure 3 *One Fine Day* (2013 version), directed by Li Jianjun. Image courtesy of New Youth Group (Photographer: Tan Zeen)

at the back of the stage periodically interrupt the narrative flow and provide pauses for reflection. As with previous works, this production aims to document the impact of modernisation and urbanisation on the lives of ordinary citizens. Over the course of a decade, it has been adapted for different cities, each version bringing a fresh repertoire of oral histories documenting life in the city through the voice of its inhabitants. Participants have included teenagers, young professionals, middle-aged entrepreneurs, retired army officers, teachers, students, doctors, policemen, rural migrants, and middle-class office workers. The casting and design of each version underscores a sense of timeliness and immediacy, capturing diverse practices of everyday life shaped by specific contexts and affects in a distinctive temporal snapshot. Editions produced during and after the COVID-19 emergency have thus shifted the focus from accounts of urban transformation since the economic reforms to stories of lockdown, social distancing, and frontline medical care, which together speak to the unique temporality of crisis of the pandemic.

The second instalment, *Popular Mechanics* (*Dazhong lixue*), premiered in 2018, turns from telling personal stories to living out one's 'acting dreams' (*biaoyan meng*), as Li Jianjun explains in a video interview (Drama Dongcheng, 2021). The production delves into the notion of amateur or non-professional acting (*suren biaoyan*) to explore everyday experiences of performance. As described in the synopsis produced for the premiere at the 2018 Wuzhen Theatre Festival, the creative concept revolves around the mechanisms that compel ordinary people to step out of their daily routines and temporarily embody aspirational alter-egos in a public role-playing fantasy; the empathy their performance elicits from the audience and each other; and the implications of their contrasting histories and personalities on the boundaries between self and role, the real and the performative. In contrast to the collective cacophony of *One Fine Day*, *Popular Mechanics* is a montage of individual performances. After a brief self-introduction, each participant presents an excerpt from a play, film, or other text of their choice that resonates with their life journey and current circumstances. At each scene change, each performer interviews the person before them about their motivation for being on stage and what they consider to be the most successful performance of their life. Each solo is framed by time-marking sound effects – a beeping watch, a ticking clock, or a horn. This temporal device both lends a sense of ritual to the proceedings and evokes the format of game shows and the culture of instant celebrity on social media platforms.

The group's collective 'performance consciousness' (*biaoyan yishi*), as Li describes it in the same interview, reflects China's shifting mass culture and media landscape. It draws attention to the ways in which media-generated models shape personal identities and lifestyles, and the impact of the technological production and consumption of culture on social dynamics and collective futures – a theme that will be explored more fully in the final part of the trilogy, *A Brief History of Human Evolution* (Renlei jianshi), premiered in 2019 (see Section 4). Moreover, the director suggests, *Popular Mechanics* can be understood as an archaeology of performance history, since each individual's textual choices and interpretations tend to resonate with the dominant genres and acting styles that have defined a particular generation or social cohort. Thus, it also traces a record of China's evolving approaches to performance over time. The excerpts illustrate the diverse influences that shape personal acting fantasies and media imaginaries. These include a rendition of *The Red Lantern* by a pensioner who grew up with the *yangbanxi*, Nina's monologue about being a 'real' actress from Anton Chekhov's *The Seagull*, the Soviet film *Lenin in 1918*, the song 'The Fools Who Dream' from the Hollywood musical romance *La La Land*, a hearing-impaired performer recreating a scene from Andrei Tarkovsky's *Mirror* in sign language, a migrant worker and a graduate student letting loose with Hong Kong comedies, and an eight-year-old child pondering Macbeth's 'Life's but a walking shadow'. As Li explains, a strong 'sense of temporality' (*shijian gan*) underpins the production, both in its pacing and in its presentation of a distilled image of society and its times, revealing the traces that life leaves behind 'from day to day, to the last syllable of recorded time', to quote Shakespeare's soliloquy.

Wang Mengfan's choreographic practice provides another compelling illustration of a reality-based *juchang* that values the expressive capacities of everyday bodies in action across social and generational divides. Her first three works, *50/60 – Dance Theatre with Dama* (50/60 – Ayimen de wudao juchang, premiered in 2015; hereafter *50/60*), *The Divine Sewing Machine* (Shensheng fengrenji, premiered in 2017; hereafter *Sewing Machine*), and *When My Cue Comes, Call Me, and I Will Answer* (Gai wo shangchang de shihou, jiao wo, wo hui huida, premiered in 2019; hereafter *When My Cue Comes*) confront conventional perceptions of the amateur bodies of public square dancers, the spontaneous bodies of children, and the ageing bodies of retired ballet professionals, respectively. Wang's approach challenges normative views of dance by embracing natural, 'imperfect' bodies as vessels of untapped expressive potential. Her creative philosophy departs from the traditional focus on physical perfection and technical virtuosity to reimagine dance as a method of understanding the body and 'a way of thinking': 'What can dance be? What can we do with dance? It may not have much to do with the kind of dance that people generally think should be on the stage. [. . .] I hope to give the audience a sense of "this is dance"' (Zen Experimental Theatre, 2020). Wang's works combine the documentation of postsocialist realities inherent in my definition of dramaturgies of the quotidian with the mnemonic and corporeal archives that characterise postsocialist performance hauntologies. By probing the impact of socialist mass culture, education, and academic dance training on the Chinese body, these productions echo the attempts of artists such as Wen Hui with *RED* (see Section 2) to trace the legacies of revolutionary ideology and body politics in the corporeal manifestations of the postrevolutionary present.

50/60 marks Wang's first foray into a choreography of the real based on the exploration of cultural memory and collective identities mediated by the body. Wang recruited a group of six women in their late fifties and sixties from among the hundreds of *guangchang wu* enthusiasts who enliven Beijing's squares and parks but are often perceived as a public nuisance. The director-choreographer bonded with the women over an extended period of time through workshops and daily activities, gently guiding them to tap into their natural bodies and find dance in spontaneous everyday actions rather than choreographed performance (Figure 4). The imprint of the quotidian on their stage movements is tangible, revealed in simple gestures such as walking, dressing, combing hair, and doing housework. The softness and natural simplicity of the movement and music contrast sharply with the fast-paced routines and boisterous soundtracks typical of *guangchang wu.* The women take the stage not as a stereotypical crowd of dancing *dama* (a common but rather pejorative term for middle-aged and elderly women), but as themselves,

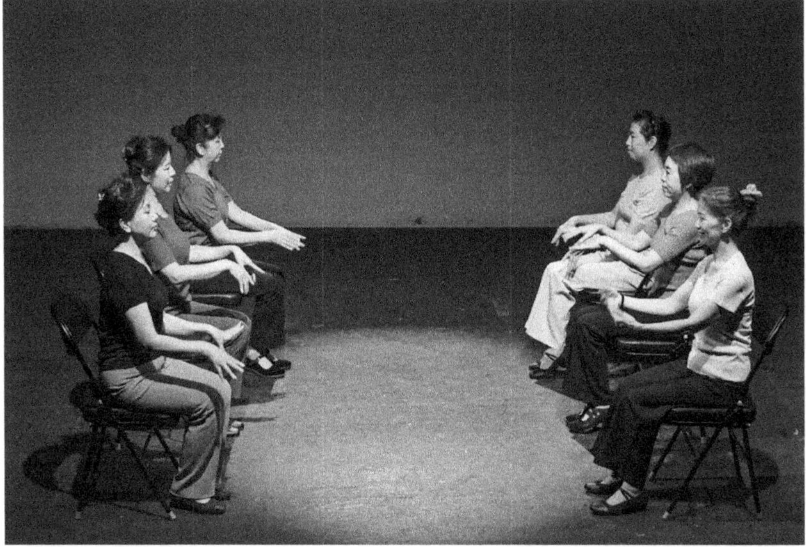

Figure 4 *50/60 – Dance Theatre with Dama* (2015). Image courtesy of Wang Mengfan (Photographer: Dazhuang)

as ordinary individuals. Their postures reflect both the mundane experiences of their personal lives and a broader generational identity rooted in a specific historical context of Chinese womanhood.

Guangchang wu represents both a distinctly postsocialist engagement with public space and a legacy of the revolutionary mass culture of the Mao era, as noted in Section 2. Just as the corporeal politics of the model ballets condition the bodies of the older dancers in *RED*, the bodies of the square dancers project a corporeal habitus shaped by collectivist modes of socialisation and political mobilisation during their youth. These include socialist-era group dances and exercise programmes, as well as embodied political rituals such as the 'loyalty dance' (*zhongzi wu*), a modernised folk dance associated with the cult of Mao during the Cultural Revolution. On the one hand, as the production synopsis explains, this shared mnemonic heritage informs the women's 'constructions of self-identity' and conceptions of dance, as evidenced by the collective dance phenomenon 'that is haunting the nation again today'. On the other hand, the choreography 'reveals how their bodies have been shaped by different aesthetics, ideologies and cultures', as it integrates elements from different dance traditions – from Chinese opera and folk dance to revolutionary ballet and ballroom dancing – within a contemporary dance theatre framework.[10] The kinaesthetic archive of an older generation of women thus serves as a historical record of profound cultural changes and evolving perceptions of the body across the temporal threshold from socialism to postsocialism, from the perspective of a director born in the 1990s and through the evolution of dance styles and entertainment forms over half a century.

Real bodies in motion are also central to Wang's second work, inspired by Samuel Beckett's description of Johann S. Bach's music as 'a divine sewing machine'. Premiered in Beijing in 2017 and revived with a new cast in Shanghai in 2018, the piece features thirteen schoolchildren performing a collage of game-like segments interspersed with Bach's compositions and a text that incorporates quotations from *Waiting for Godot*. *Sewing Machine* aims to dismantle the ideological conditioning imposed on children's bodies through linguistic and physical routines that stifle creativity and independent thought. The starting point is *langdu qiang*, a form of rehearsed recitation prevalent in primary education, which relies on emphatic 'reading aloud' (*langdu*). This formulaic pedagogy affects not only verbal articulation, but also body posture and the recursive reproduction of 'taught, rehearsed emotions', as the synopsis notes. The project therefore encourages children to revisit this practice without

[10] The synopses quoted in this section and video excerpts from the three productions are available on Wang's Vimeo channel (https://vimeo.com/mengfanwang).

the constraints of dogmatic rules and physical discipline, by embracing a vernacular dramaturgy that cultivates free self-expression in natural movement and the unrehearsed language of games and play.

Sewing Machine taps into children's unique appreciation of dance to reveal 'a way of looking at the world' that balances 'solemnity and absurdity', according to a creative statement on the production. Wang's team and the young actors devised play-based scenarios that presented alternative modes of 'reading aloud' beyond the performative emotions imposed by adults. The children explored individual performance styles to create 'their own dance' within 'a reality that is theirs alone' (The Name Time Tries to Erase, 2018a). Commenting on the performance, Japanese director Yuta Hagiwara quotes Wang's assertion that 'theatre is a place where human vulnerability can be protected', underscoring 'the beauty of vulnerability' and sense of 'fragile beauty' that this piece conveys. At the heart of the action are the 'fragile bodies' of children engaged in seemingly trivial games. But these 'fragile things', Hagiwara argues, can claim a presence on stage precisely 'because the creators first accepted their existence [. . .] without separating theatre from life' (The Name Time Tries to Erase, 2018b).

When My Cue Comes deepens the exploration of the latent potential of vulnerable bodies by delving into the realities of physical ageing among professional dancers. In this project, Cao Zhiguang and Liu Guilin – both retired from the National Ballet of China, and aged eighty-one and fifty-eight at the time of the premiere at the 2019 Wuzhen Theatre Festival – step into the unfamiliar territory of dance theatre as they seek to reconcile with their changing bodies.[11] Wang observes that, unlike amateur square dancers and children, former ballet dancers 'can control their bodies more consciously' (2020: 66). However, this control also makes them more consciously resistant to breaking free from the somatic memory embedded in their past: 'Ballet, as the form through which they have shaped their bodies, also constrains their minds,' Wang writes (72). Decades of rigorous training within an institutional system steeped in ideological conceptions of art continue to condition their sense of purpose and identity in the present. As noted in the synopsis, the dancers consciously or unconsciously strive to replicate the corporeal memory of their younger selves moulded by classical and revolutionary ballet, even as this memory clashes with their present abilities. The experience of 're-read[ing] their bodies' is thus described as an awakening from living in the past.

[11] Wang appeared on stage with the dancers in a new version developed in 2020–21 under the slightly different title *When My Cue Comes . . .* (Gai wo shangchang zhi hou), which reconstructed the creative process of the original production. This was also Cao's last performance before his passing in 2022.

The performance documents the dancers' struggle with the 'historical traces' (Wang, 2020: 68) imprinted on their once powerful, youthful, and agile bodies by revolutionary politics, and their gradual acceptance of imperfect movements and more mundane forms of bodily expression that better suit their current physical condition. Initially ambivalent and resistant to change, they eventually reconnect with their new bodies. Perceived physical 'limitations' (66) and mental blocks resulting from the sobering realisation that they can no longer master flawless ballet postures become creative strengths, as imperfections in their appearance and movement acquire hitherto untapped expressive power. The project invites both performers and audiences to overcome systemic conditioning and ageist standards of beauty in order to rethink what their bodies can achieve and how they can dance beyond technical and aesthetic canons. The enduring marks of the past are revealed as the dancers tentatively perform standard ballet steps, seeking a balance that they can barely maintain. But as they change costumes in front of the audience, symbolically shedding their old skins, they discover unexpected gestures and emotions in their 'flawed' bodies and gradually come to embrace their real bodies, now freed from self-imposed constraints, as still capable of real dance (Figure 5). At one point, Cao slips a tutu skirt over his distended belly and slaps his partner's loose muscles as she attempts a ballet pose. In another scene, Liu throws herself into a vigorous hair-whipping action, forsaking the rigid conventions of ballet for the free-flowing,

Figure 5 *When My Cue Comes, Call Me, and I Will Answer* (2019). Image courtesy of Wang Mengfan (Photographer: Wu Shi)

intuitive dance of her natural body. Throughout the performance, the two exchange words that reflect their inner conflict and newfound confidence. As they boldly take the stage without hiding behind heroic roles, flattering costumes, or beautifying make-up, their ageing bodies mark both a moment of rejuvenation in the national ballet tradition and a touching affirmation of personal self-empowerment.

'The body can be flawed,' Wang writes, 'and in my theatre it is even more "fragile". In reality, this kind of body is shunned by people and suppressed by the environment in which we live. But I see beauty in that vulnerability' (2020: 74). Wang ascribes a political value to the presence of real, ordinary bodies on the stage, because 'groups of people with no voice, no freedom or space to express themselves gain the right to speak in such a public space as theatre. This, for me, is political' (Li *et al.*, 2022: 40). To return to Li Jianjun's statement cited previously, like the nameless mankind in the New Youth Group's theatre of the ordinary, the vernacular bodies in Wang's dance theatre of real people capture the confluence of 'the everyday' and 'the extraordinary' that defines China's postsocialist dramaturgies of the quotidian.

3.3 Performing Ruins: Environments, Objects, and Bodies

The motif of the ruin as a prominent postsocialist trope has been extensively explored in studies of Chinese film and visual culture (see Ortells-Nicolau, 2017; Li, 2020), and is equally pervasive in performance. Li Jianjun conceives the ruin as 'a metaphor for the real world' and a 'dimension of time' that shapes the present as an entangled temporal site of both demolition and construction (2015: 22). The ubiquity of dilapidated environments, discarded objects, and damaged bodies in contemporary dramaturgies of the real reflects the ontological residuality of postsocialism as a transitional temporal regime that registers the incessant advance of the present and the inexorable decline of the past while holding onto its ruins. Material, emotional, and corporeal ruination salvages the relics of socialism, such as abandoned industrial sites, rusty machinery, and dusty commodities, while hoarding the psychophysical detritus scattered across the tracks and cracks of the postsocialist neoliberal race: the omnipresent rubble and wastescapes, the dislocated bodies of economic migrants and dispossessed citizens, and the injured bodies of factory workers. The collision of ruined environments, objects, and bodies reveals the harsh reality of a volatile social ecology.

The *ruined environment* appears as a central design element in the reality-based aesthetic of the New Youth Group's early works. Authentic demolition ruins were incorporated into the set of the 2011 production of *A Madman's*

Diary (Kuangren riji). The imposing debris not only visually complemented the fragmented textual rendering of Lu Xun's seminal 1918 short story, but also conveyed a notion of contemporary reality as a transitory state of simultaneous decay and development, where 'all the people living in ruins' struggle to survive and aspire to the future (Li, 2015: 22). Similarly, Li Ning and the Physical Guerrillas have attracted both acclaim and controversy for their extreme performances in improvised public spaces and found locations, including road junctions, congested highways, rooftops, bridges, demolition sites, garbage dumps, and car cemeteries, as seen in *Tape*. Abandoned industrial areas served as canvases for 'landscape sketching' in preparation for works such as *The Hidden Landscapes* (Bei yinni de fengjing), performed in 2010 in a disused chemical plant, and the Industrial Trilogy (Gongye sanbuqu), consisting of *Dictionary of Soul* (Linghun cidian), *Inch of Land* (Fangcun), and *CS-03*, premiered in 2015, 2017, and 2018, respectively. Landscape sketching parallels body sketching, aiming to uncover the 'implied meaning and attributes' of a chosen space (Li, 2013: 128). In *Dictionary of Soul*, tense physical interactions within the confines of a monumental steel frame expose the dehumanising effects of the factory regime; a construction site for a tower made of wooden planks and steel pipes sets the scene for *Inch of Land*; and the derelict workshops of the steel factory that inspired *CS-03* evoke the decline of heavy industry in northeast China. The remnants of urban decay and environmental ruins left by the Maoist industrial past serve as potent reminders of the zombification of the contemporary workforce on the capitalist assembly line, as well as the social spectrality of their socialist-era predecessors: the laid-off workers of now-defunct state-owned enterprises, once hailed as the masters of the nation, whose futures have been foreclosed in the market-driven economy of the postsocialist present.

The *ruined object* also emerges as a dominant visual cipher in post-millennial performances of the real. Prosaic materials, commodities, and discarded waste are aesthetically repurposed and imbued with spiritual attributes to signify both the vestiges of socialism and the persistent residues of postsocialist ruin. These once mundane or neglected objects are elevated to powerful symbols of historical transition, encapsulating complex layers of memory and affect. Found objects appear as both stage installations and material actors in productions by the New Youth Group, from *Metaphor of the Shadow* (Yingyu), premiered in 2012, to *A Welder's Flash* (Daidian de huohua), premiered in 2020 (see Section 4). For Li Jianjun, these objects represent relics of memory and 'remains of life' (Sohu, 2015). The director has described the voice tracks in *One Fine Day,* interspersed with the noise of firecrackers and whistling kettles, as 'sound ruins', and the mute fragments of

A Man Who Flies Up to the Sky as 'silent ruins' (Sohu, 2017). This piece, which reflects on the anxieties of modern life, is inspired by from Ilya and Emilia Kabakov's 1985 installation *The Man Who Flew into Space from His Apartment*. In the Kabakovs' work, an empty room with a hole in the ceiling, littered with scattered objects, tools, and materials, serves as a time capsule holding the 'life traces' of a man who has launched himself into space. In the set design of the New Youth Group production, a large installation composed of assorted chairs salvaged from a junk market, or 'collected from life', towers over the wooden box set. This set showcases vignettes of ordinary life in an ordinary living room, also furnished with well-worn objects (Figure 6). These mundane things – used, lived with, and then discarded as worthless – are recontextualised within the production as 'traces of time'. They draw attention to the tangible materiality of memory enclosed in the sketches of human still life within the wooden frame, itself a repurposed object made from reclaimed materials, evoking the mental image of 'a wandering private space' (Sohu, 2015). Ruined objects and settings reveal temporally layered narratives embedded in ordinariness, bearing silent witness to fleeting moments of human existence.

Figure 6 *A Man Who Flies Up to the Sky* (2015), directed by Li Jianjun. Image courtesy of New Youth Group (Photographer: Wang Renke)

Material ruins dominate the productions of the Physical Guerrillas, where everyday objects and discarded materials transcend their functional origin to become performative entities imbued with spiritual depth and symbolic resonance. Discarded machines, tools, and mechanical components reflect the dehumanisation of the factory regime and the violence of capitalism in the Industrial Trilogy. Edible materials are integral to the corporeal exploration of *Preparing* (Zhunbei), premiered in 2010, while exuberant plastic and uncanny mannequin parts provide a jarring counterpoint to the human body in the 2011 production of *The Freeze/Satellite* (Bingdongqi/Weixing), serving as a potent commentary on environmental degradation, overconsumption, and material and human expendability. In *Tape*, ritualistic interactions with mundane commodities such as tape, glue, and plaster – together with site-specific interventions set against an imposing backdrop of rubble and garbage and the arresting soundscape of traffic, sirens, roaring engines, and bulldozers – powerfully convey the destabilising effects of rampant demolition, forced relocation, and the violent disintegration of neighbourhoods during the construction boom that preceded the 2008 Olympic Games and the 2009 National Games in Jinan and other locations in Shandong. In the situationist choreographies that structure this multi-site project, the company performs amidst polluted traffic, debris, car wrecks, and urban waste. Newspapers, plastic, and assorted refuse are taped and glued to their bodies and film equipment. As they evade police or confront hostile onlookers, their guerrilla actions communicate a pervasive sense of alarm, urgency, and precariousness. In these performances, tape is not only an extension of the body and an aesthetic material, but also fulfils its practical functions, sealing the doors of buildings slated for demolition and the belongings of displaced citizens. As such, the ruined object emerges as a symbolic binder, holding together the physical and psychological wreckage of an urban space in the throes of reconstruction. It is also a signifier of social resilience and a tenacious clinging to a sense of cohesion in the midst of a life in tatters.

The *ruined body* is another ubiquitous trope of socio-existential disaffection in postsocialist conditions. In *Tape*, still, performative actions among ruins are intercut with media coverage of the Olympics and construction plans for the upcoming National Games. Official performances of postsocialism are thus televised as the progressive master temporality of the state performs itself live on camera. The healthy, disciplined bodies of athletes and the beautified bodies of happy newlyweds on the day of the opening ceremony are offset by the damaged, dishevelled bodies of rebel artists and unruly citizens as inconvenient 'social debris' (Hillenbrand, 2023: 3). We see the injured body of Li Ning, bleeding from a cut foot during a nude *pas de deux* with a bulldozer on the rubble; the disabled body of a Physical Guerrillas performer; the violated bodies of citizens evicted from their homes and businesses – forcibly restrained, coerced into compliance, or ready to self-immolate in protest; and the unseemly, campy bodies of performers amidst debris and machinery, mocking the rituals of the state and consumer society with garbage stuck to their skin, hair, and clothes. On the day the Olympic torch passes through Jinan, the company stages a carnivalesque ersatz torch relay and a mock fashion show on a landfill site. Some performers stutter as if on a catwalk, adorned with plastic bottles, blister packs, and e-waste, while another squats on the ground, eating from a plastic bag, in a grotesque cross between model and ragpicker.

Hillenbrand identifies the ragpicker as an emblem of precarity and 'an artist of the dump' (95) – a figure that looms large in documentary film and visual culture. Similarly, Grass Stage's *Little Society* portrays ruined embodiments of social exclusion and capitalist exploitation in a series of vignettes featuring a ragpicker, a beggar, and a sex worker that lay bare the ugly banality of survival. The ragpicker bounces around a wasteland of plastic bottles arranged to replicate a degraded miniature cityscape, her body tucked into a large garbage sack. She fills the sack with crushed bottles until she disappears inside it, swallowed by the garbage and becoming garbage herself. In an ironic twist, she sings 'our future is in the fields of hope' (from the popular song 'In the Fields of Hope' ('Zai xiwang de tianye shang'), famously performed by Xi Jinping's wife, Peng Liyuan), before collapsing to the ground and being dragged off the stage, tossed aside like worthless junk.[12]

World Factory presents an equally grim catalogue of human wreckage. The depleted bodies of displaced migrant workers and the emotional wounds of their left-behind children starkly reveal the physical and psychological toll of postsocialist economic development. Disfigured and crippled bodies highlight the issue of industrial injury, with depictions of hands maimed on the assembly line and accounts of the physical and mental agony caused by exposure to toxic fumes and pollution. The expendable bodies of suicidal workers, scorned in a callous dialogue between the characters of a clown and a psychologist, recall the notorious spate of suicides at Foxconn beginning in 2010. The lyrics of a song in memory of these workers and the harrowing poetic imagery of the worker-poet Xu Lizhi, who ended his life in 2014 at the age of twenty-four, add weight to the production's indictment of the devastating consequences of the neoliberal dream. The disembodied silhouettes of blue paper dolls, carelessly cut and discarded by the performers, stand in for the objectified bodies of blue-collar workers, pointing to the dehumanisation

[12] For a video excerpt, see Grass Stage (2009).

of individuals within the world factory system, which, as the character of an environmental expert declares in the play, 'is actually nothing but a world garbage dump!' (Zhao Chuan and Grass Stage, 2022: 84).[13]

4 Performing Postsocialist Futurities

The third regime of temporality revolves around the future. It addresses performative responses to the postsocialist condition through the projection of 'futural orientations', a term coined by anthropologists Rebecca Bryant and Daniel Knight (2019) to conceptualise future-oriented sensibilities. The corresponding category of *postsocialist futurities* denotes performances that articulate a preoccupation with the future, imagining future scenarios, futuristic visions, and alternate human and posthuman realities. These futures may emerge as counterpoints to troubled pasts or as symptoms of the indeterminacy of the present, revealing 'how presents and pasts are always and inevitably shaped by the ends for which we strive' (20). Temporal manifestations of futurity can take various forms: from dystopian predictions, posthuman allegories, and technophobic prophecies of digital doom to nostalgic musings, expectant utopias, ambivalent heterotopias, and virtual fantasies of escape. These multiple dimensions of the future transcend the restrictive confines of official blueprints for China's future and optimistic slogans envisioning a 'community of common destiny for mankind' (*renlei mingyun gongtongti*). They carve out a space for exploring broader possibilities of postsocialist futurity that go beyond the ideological engineering of technocratic utopias and the progressive temporality enshrined in nation-state futurologies. Essentially, performances of postsocialist times as futural orientations offer an analytical compass for navigating 'the indefinite teleologies of everyday life' (Bryant and Knight, 2019: 19).

Just as the association between futurity and technology is entrenched in both official discourse and popular consciousness, practices of future-making in the realm of performance are frequently intertwined with technological innovation and imagination. China's rapid technological advancement has gone hand in hand with postsocialist economic growth in a state of accelerated temporality and spatiotemporal compression. This dynamic has generated a keen awareness of the potentials and pitfalls of technology in shaping individual and collective futures. In performance, technology emerges as both a tool and a theme for the future. On the one hand, postsocialist performance manifests technologically inflected futurities by aestheticising technology and exploring innovative technical apparatuses such as live cinema, livestreams, interactive formats, and immersive experiences. On the other hand, performance dramatises technology

[13] For a video recording of the Shenzhen performance, see Grass Stage (2014).

as *the* future by staging future worlds infused with technology. This section therefore considers applications and visions of technology in the construction of the future through theatre, and possible models for a postsocialist theatre of the future. It examines live and online productions by the New Youth Group and Théâtre du Rêve Expérimental that negotiate postsocialist realities through technological innovation and imaginings of techno-futures. The propositions of futurity that emerge from these works further illustrate the heterochronic configuration of postsocialism – envisioning possible futures while drawing on textual and mnemonic repositories from the past to respond to present conditions.

4.1 Where Are We Going: Postsocialist Performance and Futurity

In October 2019, Théâtre du Rêve Expérimental premiered the site-specific production *Where Do We Come From, What Are We, Where Are We Going 2.0* (Women cong hechu lai, women shi shei, women xiang hechu qu 2.0) at the Wuzhen Theatre Festival. This interactive 'micro-theatre' performance allowed four audience members to walk through a courtyard, guided by audio cues. Each participant simultaneously experienced and became a character in four different narratives about immigration featuring a pig, a pregnant mosquito, a sea turtle, and a fugitive Edward Snowden. A text featured in the production trailer asks: 'Who are you? Where were you born? Where have you been? [. . .] What kind of person do you want to become? What kind of world do you wish the world to become?' (Théâtre du Rêve Expérimental, 2019). The futural structure of feeling evoked by these questions permeates the heterochronic quality of post-socialist performance more broadly as a manifestation of the composite temporality of postsocialism, grounded in the present and affecting present actions while projecting imaginaries forward and backward in time.

As discussed in Section 1, Xi's political rhetoric has reoriented nation-state temporalities, affirming continuity with Marxist-Maoist thought and the revival of imperial heritage alongside cutting-edge technological investment as central to shaping China's future (Lanza, 2023: 609). However, the Xi era marks not only a time of dreams of national rejuvenation and global leadership, but also one of economic instability, environmental degradation, increased social surveillance, and technocratic governance. This regime of the future past or 'future anterior' – potentially 'a future undoing of its past achievement', as Nick Browne (1994: 7) famously wrote of Hong Kong's cultural anxiety over the 1997 handover – has reconfigured earlier notions of postsocialism and its cultural-artistic responses in the new millennium.

In *Sinophone Utopias*, Andrea Riemenschnitter, Jessica Imbach, and Justyna Jaguścik argue that postmillennial cultural constructions of the future present more diverse and nuanced imaginaries than the nostalgic, dystopian, and futureless visions of the late twentieth century (2022: 1). Acknowledging the discrepancy between the CCP's rhetorical utopianism and 'a broad range of dystopian realities' on the ground, they draw on Michael Marder and Patricia Vieira's notion of 'existential utopia' and Derrida's concept of the promise to explore 'the productive aspects of negation in dystopian narratives' and 'post-utopian cultural representations', as well as the emancipatory potential of the past in imagining futures to come (3–4). Essays by Jaguścik and Paola Iovene in the same volume interpret works by Grass Stage and the New Workers Art Troupe as grassroots micro-utopias, offering enactments of alternative futures that counter official futurology. While in Section 3 I situate both collectives within a discourse of precarity anchored in the temporal regime of the present, Jaguścik (2022) highlights *World Factory*'s appeal to utopian socialism against capitalist exploitation and its proposal of a counter-utopia for a more sustainable and equitable future community.

The applicability of multiple temporal categories to a single production once again underscores the entanglements of postsocialist temporalities and the embeddedness of futural orientations in the timespace of the present – what Bryant and Knight call 'the futur*alism* of everyday life' (2019: 12). Such utopias may not materialise, as suggested by the ragpicker's singing act in *Little Society*, which seems to mock the future as a failure of the present. But they still afford a vision of subaltern futurity as 'the capacity to aspire' (Appadurai, 2013: 179) to emancipatory alterities, rather than sinking into 'utopian ruins', to borrow Li Jie's (2020) phrase. The typologies of postsocialist futurities examined here, however, also include a repertoire of anti-utopias, foreshadowing futures that are hauntingly reminiscent of the present. These can manifest as dystopias, as seen in the New Youth Group's *Brief History of Human Evolution* (hereafter *Brief History*), or as refusals of utopia, as in the online production of *Waiting for Godot* (Dengdai Geduo 2.0 ban; hereafter *Godot*), directed by Wang Chong during the COVID-19 pandemic. Yet other works, such as the New Youth Group's digital documentary performance *A Welder's Flash* (hereafter *Welder*), also livestreamed during the pandemic, project futurity into virtual realms of heterotopia.

4.2 Techno-Dystopia: The Future as the Death of the Real

Brief History anchors the postsocialist theatre of the real to the technological imagination of the future. It expands *Popular Mechanics*' reflection on the evolution of personal and collective models with the evolution of media and popular culture, addressing the relationship between humanity and technology, self and image, the real world and worlds generated by images. The cast includes twenty-five nonprofessional performers who immerse themselves in a collective role-playing game, testing the boundaries between real and simulated selves to explore the mediated perception and reproduction of individual self-identities and public idols through technologies of image-making. Compared to earlier works in the Amateur Trilogy, however, *Brief History* presents a far more pronounced futural orientation. The emphasis is no longer on the investigation of the ordinary as a revelation of the authenticity of the real, but on the prefiguration of the future as the death of the real, proffering a negative prophecy of the human future as a techno-dystopia.

The performances at the 2019 Wuzhen Theatre Festival took place in an arena equipped with computers and large overhead screens facing the audience seated on four sides. The actors opened image files stored on the computers, which were projected onto the screens. This setup created a 360-degree media panopticon, reflecting the ubiquity of displays and imaging devices in contemporary society. They then engaged in 'imitation performances' (*mofang biaoyan*) of over one hundred images displayed sequentially on the screens, first individually, then in quartets, and finally as a full ensemble, implementing a performance method that Li Jianjun has described as 'image karaoke' (*tuxiang kalaOK*) or 'choreography with images' (*yong yingxiang bianwu*) (Li H., 2019) (Figure 7). The images used in the production were selected from a large library of photographs and videos sourced online and contributed by participants in casting workshops held prior to

Figure 7 *A Brief History of Human Evolution* (2019), directed by Li Jianjun. Image courtesy of New Youth Group (Photographer: Yuan Wei)

the premiere. The nature and sequence of the images – from analogue to digital, from still to moving image, from animation to gaming – gives them a distinctive temporal value, framing the history and memory of individuals and humanity within a history of technology.

Brief History draws heavily on Baudrillard's vision of the hyperreal as the disappearance of the real into 'an allegory of death' (1988: 144–45) and its 'artificial resurrection' through mediated reproduction (167). It questions the impact of technology on the experience of the real and its implications for human progress and the future of humanity in a media-saturated reality. Everyday reality is reconfigured as a hyperreality shaped by endlessly reproducible simulacra, where the boundaries between reality and simulation are blurred, and the simulated becomes indistinguishable from the real. Humanity is left with the '*the desert of the real*' (166), seemingly consigned to a future of digital doom. Li himself invites such an interpretation in an interview given at the time of the premiere. The director mentions the emergence of the 'caricature self' as a consequence of the demise of the 'real self', as the mediatised world supersedes the real world (Li H., 2019). This statement ostensibly invokes Baudrillard's definition of cultural consumption 'as the time and place of the caricatural resurrection, the parodic evocation of what already no longer exists – of what is not so much "consumed" as "consummated" (completed, past and gone)' (1998: 99). What is past and gone here is the authentic perception of the real, replaced by a '*hallucinatory resemblance to itself*' (1988: 145) in the hyperreality of images. Media generate reality, transform reality, and change our awareness of reality and ourselves. They produce ideal selves, especially with the proliferation of participatory formats such as reality television and digital social networks, which have enabled enhanced performances of the self. Image curation and image sharing have become routine, and we are constantly surrounded by images. 'Reality transformed by images has become our daily life,' Li continues. 'To some extent, "reality" has died, and we have been changed.' The exploration of everyday reality as constructed by images thus becomes the starting point for exploring human history and the 'living self' through a 'history of images' (Li H., 2019).

The performance begins with a sequence dealing with personal history and individual memory. Here, the performers are still treading on the territory of the real, albeit in a mediated form, as the images that they introduce and imitate capture lived experiences. These are private photographs documenting individual pasts: childhood memories, family portraits, school pictures, souvenirs of memorable journeys, and other significant life events. Each person mimics the pose of an image selected from their private archive, providing a backstory about its origins. They then momentarily freeze in the depicted posture, evoking the typical gestures of *yangbanxi* heroes and the classical Chinese theatre (*xiqu*) convention of 'striking a pose' (*liangxiang*), or still frames in screen-based media. Others then join in a collective imitation of the individual's memory image. This section introduces the theme of mediated memory, underscoring the vital function of image-making technologies in carrying the past 'as a memory cloud', as described in the synopsis produced for the Wuzhen premiere. These human 'inventions' – from analogue photography and film to digital imaging and videography – are both markers of human progress and 'performers' in their own right. Images and bodies that 'write history with their gestures' serve as temporal connectors between past, present, and future. But images are also reminders of the mortality of bodies. Unlike human bodies, images neither age nor die, preserving their history and memory forever in the ageless temporality of a timeless future.

The next segment delves into collective history and shared memory. Each performer presents and imitates a personal idol (*ouxiang*). The image catalogue includes politicians, scientists, entertainers, athletes, and other public icons spanning an entire century. There are also video interviews with passers-by answering questions about who their idols are and which public figures they love or hate. Most are real-life models, highlighting prosthetic memories internalised and appropriated through the technologies of mass culture. But there are also nonhuman idols, including superheroes and characters from comics, anime, and computer games, marking a gradual shift in the history of human evolution into the media-generated realities and virtual worlds of the hyperreal. The performance then transitions into a collective choreography centred on images of public figures. The images highlight the performative quality of media appearances. The performers engage in exaggerated imitations of various celebrities and popular icons, who in turn perform for the cameras and their audiences. At the same time, this configuration evokes collective forms of social performance and everyday leisure activities such as karaoke singing, public square dancing, and social media livestreaming. Their hyperbolic postures again invite a Baudrillardian interpretation. As the performers participate in a collective mimicry of simulacra – 'a participation which can only be enacted through a *liturgy*, a formal code of signs meticulously voided of all meaning content' (Baudrillard, 1998: 104) – their actions transcend mere imitation and become, in fact, simulations.

The final sequence presents a dystopian vision of technological alienation, where individual personalities succumb to a homologated future, or no future at all. The performers don identical headsets to become virtual avatars, signifying the erosion of subjectivity in the realm of the hyperreal, or the gamification of the real, after 'reality has passed over into the play of reality' (Baudrillard, 1988:

146). A montage of war imagery from films, games, and actual battlefields introduces a collective game-like simulation of combat that culminates in the apparent extinction of human civilisation, as the players shoot each other until they all fall dead on the ground in the darkness. The game is over. After the lights come back on, however, the actors stand up, retake the pose from their personal photograph shown in the opening sequence, and then walk out one by one to the cue of the Super Mario Bros. theme song, leaving their headsets behind, as if to suggest the final resuscitation of the caricature self back into the real self. Ultimately, *Brief History* seeks to answer the question: 'Is technology toxic?' Li argues that technology has altered human consciousness to the extent that people strive to become replicas of the idols they see in the media:

> The earliest humans transformed the world by imitating reality, but today, the symbolic world we create through imitation has in turn transformed us. This is what we call 'technological toxicity'. We combine the performance of the actors with a variety of technical means on stage to present some 'toxic' landscapes. In addition, we hope to explore a 'detoxification' path through creation. We also hope to make the audience think about 'what is progress': Does technology shape human beings, or does it destroy them? (Li H., 2019)

Li's statement illustrates the classic binary of utopia and dystopia that, as Tom Boellstorff suggests, has routinely informed reflections on human futures in relation to technological development. Historically, the advent of new technologies has been perceived either as revolutionary, even salvific, or as a threat to humanity. However, Boellstorff argues, 'the relative subsidence of such utopian and dystopian narratives often indicates that a technology is no longer seen as such, but has become a mundane tool for living' (2014: 743–44). As detailed in the next section, the mundanity of technology as an essential 'tool for living' would soon take on new significance – indeed, urgency – with the onset of the COVID-19 pandemic. A critical juncture in the history of human evolution led to the creation of works that attempted to navigate this binary, embracing the positive potential of technology even as they continued to probe its alienating aspects.

4.3 Pandemic Temporalities, Online Theatre, and the Theatre of the Future

In *The Anthropology of the Future*, Bryant and Knight (2019) identify six 'futural orientations' – anticipation, expectation, speculation, potentiality, hope, and destiny – as analytical tools for understanding how imagining the future informs action in the present. This framework underpins my analysis of online performances produced between the onset of the Wuhan lockdown in early 2020 and the relaxation of China's zero-COVID restrictions in late 2022.

These aesthetic actions reflect an altered perception of time in response to the pandemic present. As Siobhan Kattago notes, the pandemic emergency transformed the ordinary perception of time into a ghostly experience of temporal distortion and suspension. On the one hand, people were 'caught between linear time (*chronos*) and rupture (*kairos*)', and on the other in 'an extended present' shaped by 'the boundless and limbo-like time of eternity' (*aion*) (2021: 1401). The viral temporality of COVID-19 marked 'a *crisis chronotope*' that nevertheless fostered '*mnemonic mobility*' (Parui and Raj, 2021: 1431) and affective connections in virtual realms, despite the absence of actual movement and physical contact.

Futural impulses driven by technological innovation took on sudden urgency with the outbreak of the pandemic. The closure of physical venues and stringent public health measures fuelled a new digital imperative, prompting a shift towards remote production. Online festivals, interactive settings, and participatory interventions on livestreaming platforms and digital social media became the status quo. But what began as a remedial response to an exceptional situation became a catalyst for new modes of production and spectatorship. Emergency experiments laid the groundwork for future aesthetic innovations and proposals for the future of theatre, or a theatre of the future. Moreover, the crisis temporality of the pandemic lent resonance to technologically mediated imaginaries of the future in uncertain and seemingly unending times.

In the early days of the pandemic, Li Jianjun gathered a group of former *Popular Mechanics* participants to produce a short online version about the experience of mandatory social distancing and self-quarantine. The cast captured snapshots of their daily lives on their mobile phones from their homes across China, and two from abroad. The performance was livestreamed during the MamaPapa Festival, which ran for two weeks in February 2020. Hosted by the Beijing Contemporary Art Foundation, the event attracted dozens of submissions spanning various art forms, all under the banner of Joseph Beuys' statement 'Everyone is an artist', which also inspired Li's concept of *fanren juchang* (see Section 3).[14] Each of the twelve individual segments that make up the twenty-four-minute piece begins with an intertitle introducing the person and their location. Domestic scenes then alternate with shots of deserted neighbourhoods, mostly filmed from windows, and diary-style intertitles in which each person describes their state of mind and daily routine during this time of seclusion and stasis. Some regret not being able to travel and celebrate the New Year with their families, while others describe strict surveillance, restrictions on movement, and shortages of essentials such as food and N95

[14] For a video recording, see Beijing Contemporary Art Foundation (2020).

masks in remote areas. Others have raised money for hospitals in Wuhan. Some testimonies are light-hearted, some resigned, some anxious, but all long for an imminent return to former life. Each segment ends with the person in front of the camera reciting Olga's final monologue in Anton Chekhov's *Three Sisters* for 'those who are also struggling and trying to survive', as Li explains in an opening intertitle that prefaces the project:

> Time will pass, and we shall depart for ever. We shall be forgotten – our faces, our voices, even how many of us there were. But our sufferings will turn to joy for those who live after us. Peace and happiness will dwell on earth, and people living now will be blessed and spoken well of. Dear sisters, our life is not ended yet. We shall live! (Chekhov, 1983: 89)

This digital iteration of *Popular Mechanics* portrays an interrupted and suspended present that is nonetheless brightened by *anticipation* and *hope*. Bryant and Knight suggest that collective anticipation intensifies in times 'of uncertain or threatening futures' (2019: 48). Anticipation alleviates the frustration and anxiety of an unpredictable present and seeks to 'normalize' it 'through a speculative imagination of the future' (43). Hope blends with anticipation as a coping mechanism in times of crisis, reconciling the present with a future in which change is awaited (153). This composite futural orientation emerges not only from the participants' accounts of resilience and efforts to forge a virtual community through remote collective performance. It is also reinforced by the ritualistic repetition of Olga's wistful lines, and her appeal to look to the future despite ongoing challenges. The sisters are trapped in the unwanted reality of an isolated provincial town, yearning for their past lives in Moscow, just as the actors and their audience are confined to their homes, longing for human connection and their own metaphorical Moscow beyond the bars of their windows.

An affective structure of frustration and confinement similarly informs Wang Chong's COVID-inflected rendition of Beckett's *Godot*, echoing the motif of waiting found in *Three Sisters* – a futural waiting in the latter, and perhaps a futile one in the former. Yet, Wang's version invites interpretation in the future tense, as a glimpse of future theatre and a gesture towards postpandemic futures. Marking China's first foray into 'Zoom theatre', *Godot* was livestreamed in two parts on 5 and 6 April 2020 on Tencent to an unprecedented 290,000 viewers. The production team and cast were based in Beijing, Datong, Guangzhou, and Wuhan. The four actors performed in real time from their homes. A notable exception was an outdoor scene shot guerrilla-style from two cars on the deserted streets of Wuhan at night, just one day before the lockdown was lifted.

A few months before the outbreak of the pandemic, Wang's aforementioned *Where Do We Come From, What Are We, Where Are We Going 2.0* premiered at the Wuzhen Theatre Festival, at the same time as *Brief History.* The audio track featured in the production trailer encourages participants to fly to uncharted destinations, echoing the director's assertion that 'Theater must go out from theater' to explore new frontiers of imagination and future potentials. As he states: 'The new era of theater has to come. The future of theater is a blank page' (Théâtre du Rêve Expérimental, 2019). The pandemic provided the occasion to fill that page, with *Godot* giving concrete form to Wang's vision. Two weeks after *Godot*'s global livestream, Wang published an 'Online Theatre Manifesto' (Xianshang xiju xuanyan) on his company's website, writing:

> Theater artists only realized that theater is non-essential once the plague was everywhere. In fact, theater became non-essential long ago. [. . .] Theater is not public forum anymore. Most theater has nothing to do with our times. [. . .] Yet the online world is public and a forum. [. . .] Online theater is absolutely not a stop-gap measure during this plague. [. . .] Human society will soon be full of virtual reality, augmented reality, artificial intelligence, and artificial organisms. So will the arts. Humans will at last redefine 'human,' and also 'theater.' Theater artists, having experienced 'the death of theater,' shouldn't and can't stand by awaiting our doom. Online theater is no death knell for theater, but a prelude to our future. (2020a)[15]

Wang heralds online theatre not just as a temporary panacea, but as a long-term 'antidote' to theatre's 'loss of essentiality' and growing estrangement from the public sphere (Chun, 2021: 313–14), thus providing a possible template for a future beyond the pandemic – one ostensibly enabled by technology. *Godot* and the Manifesto, as Tarryn Chun observes, 'offer a vision of what postpandemic theatre might become: an intermedial forum that works to counteract the nonessential nature of contemporary theatre, the negative effects of recent technological developments, and the limitations imposed/exposed by the global pandemic' (315). Wang's programmatic statement reflects the aspirational futurity fuelled by the twin impulses of technological innovation and technological imagination that, as noted previously, are distinctly perceptible in the futural mindset of the postmillennium. However, while the medium of production signals a future pregnant with potential that is almost within reach, its content points to more ambiguous and uncertain prospects that threaten to turn 'positive potentiality into negative actuality' (Bryant and Knight, 2019: 104).

Wang's version remains faithful to Beckett's text, but reimagines the aimless idling of two tramps on a desolate country road as a late-night video chat between a heterosexual couple. Fufu (Vladimir) and Ganggang (Estragon) are self-isolating in their flats in different cities, waiting for the pandemic to end. This

[15] See Wang (2020b) for the Chinese version. For video excerpts from *Godot*, see Théâtre du Rêve Experimental (2020).

time of emergency and rupture, though situated in the contingency of China's new viral reality, resonates with the anxious immobility of the original play. As Ganggang cautiously advises: 'Don't let's do anything. It's safer.' The daily boredom endured by the couple as they wander aimlessly in their pyjamas through their dreary domestic surroundings is not the only element that accentuates such chronostasis. Equally significant is the recurring design motif of clocks, either made of paper and therefore not working, or stuck at the same hour, constantly reminding them of the frozen temporality of a wait that stretches into eternity. Bozhuo (Pozzo), a businessman, is styled as the quintessential *tuwei* (earthy, tasteless, tacky, uncool) type, sporting a garish silk suit and heavy gold-plated jewellery. His underling, Xingyun'er (Lucky), peddles products online in a satirical send-up of livestream shopping, a burgeoning business model in China during the pandemic.

In the first act, a coughing fit from Bozhuo prompts the couple to reach for surgical masks and thermometers, as a tongue-in-cheek nod to the stringent government measures and hygiene protocols in place at the time. Fufu is seen wearing a beaked plague doctor's mask, a symbol of pestilence and death, and other pandemic-related paraphernalia, and routinely checking his and his family members' temperature (the actor's parents and brother were on site and visible during the livestream). In the second act, Bozhuo languishes in a hospital bed on a respirator, crying for help, while Xingyun'er experiences an exhilarating moment of physical freedom and spiritual emancipation. An actor based in Wuhan played the role. This was a deliberate casting choice to give the production a palpable contextual immediacy. With Bozhuo supposedly dying of a respiratory illness, Xingyun'er was filmed live as he drove alone towards the Yellow Crane Tower – a historical landmark that would be instantly recognisable to Chinese audiences – in a sequence that bordered on the politically sensitive as Wuhan was still under lockdown at the time (Figure 8). In this crucial moment of futural imagination, where authority collapses and the powerless take control, Xingyun'er is granted a double liberation, both from servitude to his master and from the harsh restrictions imposed by the virus – an invisible force as looming as Godot, and perhaps as ominous. The timing of the scene captured the forward-looking sense of *anticipation* for the imminent return to daily life that Wuhan residents were experiencing at the very moments of the livestream.

For Fufu and Ganggang, however, the production predicts a future that is stalled, interrupted, and postponed. Compared to the pandemic reworking of *Popular Mechanics*, *Godot* veers less intensely towards hope and more towards *speculation* about 'the immanent' and 'the unknown' (Bryant and Knight, 2019: 82). This speculative futural structure – of suspension, doubt, and uncertainty – can lead to

Figure 8 Screenshot of the online production of *Waiting for Godot* (2020), directed by Wang Chong. Image courtesy of Théâtre du Rêve Expérimental.

conjecture and deception (101) about the true nature of the anticipated future, be it the arrival of Godot or the threat of viral death. In this light, *Godot* contemplates postpandemic futurity while also intimating a latent 'collapse or exhaustion' of the future, where the hope afforded by *Popular Mechanics*' evocation of *Three Sisters* 'may turn to apathy, frustrated planning to disillusion, and imagination to fatigue' (19). Earlier, I characterised this work as a refusal of utopia not only because the uncanny suggestion of a circular future fraught with endless waiting undermines the possibility of utopian endings, as the couple are stuck in an eternal present that ends as it began – only with greater despair. Unless, of course, the elusive Godot finally appears and the postpandemic 'normal' he represents finally arrives. But also because their resolve to remain in the present – to wait for Godot, the end of the pandemic, and a return to their former lives – precludes any utopian refuge.

Just as the production's attitude towards the future is ambivalent, so too is its position on technology. From the perspective of the medium, technology holds positive potential, allowing the performance to take place and ensuring the survival of theatre during the pandemic. At the level of content, however, technology is mostly portrayed as alienating to the characters. Xingyun'er embodies a techno-induced farce of twenty-first-century capitalist alienation, enslaved by the exploitative demands of e-commerce and platform capitalism. Fufu wrestles with a smart home device voiced by a virtual assistant, who takes over the role of the Boy messenger. This substitution removes any semblance of human connection, turning Beckett's already tenuous hope of salvation into a nightmarish future in which human destiny is surrendered to artificial intelligence. Andreas Huyssen argues that the artistic perception of technological mass culture in the early twentieth century oscillated between 'the aesthetization' and 'the horror of technics'. Similarly, this production lends substance to the 'bipolar experience of technology' of advanced capitalism and viral virtuality of the early twenty-first century, 'by integrating technology and the technological imagination in the production of art' (1986: 10).

I conclude this section with a brief discussion of the New Youth Group's *Welder*. Directed by Li Jianjun, it was livestreamed on the video sharing platform Bilibili on 3 and 4 December 2020, as part of the thirteenth hybrid edition of the Beijing Fringe Festival.[16] Compared to *Brief History* and *Godot*, *Welder* shares a similar ambivalent futurity, but takes a more positive stance on the potential of technology. It thus seems to transcend the binary of utopia and dystopia noted previously in relation to *Brief History* by envisioning a virtual heterotopia. In this alternative realm, the virtual signifies a latent promise of the real rather than its demise. On the one hand, *Welder* is an extension of the Amateur Trilogy, born out of the demands of remote performance during the pandemic. It features a solo performance by Ma Jiandong, a migrant worker who participated in all three parts of the trilogy and in the 2020 webcast of *Popular Mechanics*. On the other hand, its innovative digital format anticipates the experiments with new technologies that the company would later pursue in its postpandemic Posthuman Trilogy (Hou renlei sanbuqu).[17]

In an hour-long monologue, complemented by digital film footage, live video, animation, and a tabletop object theatre, Ma recounts his family history and present circumstances, his personal story of migration from rural Hebei to Beijing, and his hopes for the future. Potatoes, corncobs, bricks, toys, tools, and other performing objects stand in for family members across three generations. These material narrative devices function as mnemonic talismans, hauntological ruins, and temporal markers, reflecting 'the "time difference" in the logic of modernization', as Li Jianjun puts it (Fake Festival, 2020), between the futureless countryside that Ma left behind at the age of sixteen and the emancipatory promise of his journey to the capital. His storytelling blends elements of magical realism with the gritty reality of life in rural China during decades of socioeconomic transformation. Supernatural tales of curses, rituals, and ghostly apparitions combine with accounts of recurring family tragedies and the decline of rural communities as the younger generations have migrated to the cities.

Ma's decision to leave the family village to work as a welder in Beijing's booming construction industry articulates futurity as *anticipation*. As Bryant and Knight argue,

---

[16] For a video excerpt, see New Youth Group (2021).

[17] The Posthuman Trilogy includes *World on a Wire* (Shijie danxi zhijian), a 2021 production based on Rainer Werner Fassbinder's sci-fi television series; *The Metamorphosis* (Bianxing ji), adapted in 2021 from Franz Kafka's novella; and *The Master and Margarita* (Dashi yu Magelite), premiered in 2022 and based on Mikhail Bulgakov's novel.

> Anticipation, then, is more than simply expecting something to happen; it is the act of looking forward that also pulls me in the direction of the future and prepares the groundwork for that future to occur. Unlike expectation, anticipation specifically contains the sense of thrusting or pressing forward, where the past is called upon in this movement toward the future. (2019: 28)

While Ma's domestic archaeology retraces the past, his present actions – the forward movement of migration to the city to chase the nation's neoliberal dream – signal an aspiration for a future that is brighter than the misery and hardship of his ancestors. His family endured a present that excluded the futural orientation of *hope*, while his generation aspired to contribute to the construction of the glitzy, globalised future embodied by iconic Olympic venues such as the Bird's Nest, which Ma and countless migrant workers like him effectively built.

Ma's fortunes took a turn for the worse in 2017, when the government launched a campaign to expel migrant workers from the capital, and declined further during the pandemic, as he also testifies in the *Popular Mechanics* webcast. Nonetheless, the final scene affords a vision of hopeful futurity, as he is seen flying over a digital map of Beijing through immersive VR technology (Figure 9). This virtual simulation represents both an escape fantasy and a liberating projection of the future he imagined when he first arrived in the city. Virtual reality gives him agency in shaping his future trajectory, as opposed to the embodied reality of his present life. The VR scenario thus activates a futural orientation of *potentiality*, namely 'the future's *capacity to become future*, or the future as virtuality in the present' (Bryant and Knight, 2019: 107). This future is not yet actual, but real nonetheless, echoing

Figure 9 *A Welder's Flash* (2020), directed by Li Jianjun. Image courtesy of New Youth Group (Screenshot by the author)

a Deleuzian notion of '*the reality of the virtual*', where the virtual signifies a 'potentiality' of the real (Massumi, 2014: 55–56). However, the production also illustrates the inherent paradox of potentiality. Potentiality contains a 'futural momentum' of *hope* as a proactive present movement that drives 'the indeterminacy of potentiality' into actuality (Bryant and Knight, 2019: 134). But it also contains a negative affect of '*impotentia*', when what is anticipated does not materialise (130). Ma's anticipatory future is a future interrupted, by precarity and the pandemic, which might become a future denied.

Ultimately, *Welder* constructs an ambiguous heterotopia that 'is capable of juxtaposing in a single real place several spaces, several sites that are in themselves incompatible' (Foucault, 1986: 25). These heterotopic spaces correspond to heterochronic 'slices in time' (26), reflecting the multiple dimensions of reality – and realism – that converge in the production: magical realism for the past, documentary realism for the present, and mediated realism for the future. By embedding strategies of the theatre of the real in analogue and digital technologies, *Welder* links the modes of documentary and embodied realism explored in the previous section with the digitally mediated realities addressed here. As such, it illustrates a crucial juncture in the development of postmillennial postdramatics, both in terms of technical innovation and in their engagement with postsocialism and its temporal entanglements. As this study has repeatedly shown, technology plays a critical role in the construction and articulation of postsocialist temporal regimes: as a hauntological apparatus, to revive spectral pasts; as a documentary device, to capture the unfolding of the real; and as a lens for future projections. Technology intervenes in the three regimes as a mediator and connector between disparate material realities and disjointed temporal orders that converge in performances of postsocialist times.

Conclusion: Performing Postsocialism, Transnationally

While this Element has focused on the repercussions of postsocialist transformation on China's performance cultures, Chinese postsocialism and its cultural reverberations are not confined to the Chinese nation. China's transition from a socialist to a neoliberal capitalist state has not only reshaped international relations and the global economy, but has also fuelled cross-cultural entanglements and imaginaries, positioning Chinese postsocialism as a transnational phenomenon with far-reaching ramifications. Echoing scholars of post-Soviet societies and formerly socialist states in Central and Eastern Europe (see Stenning and Hörschelmann, 2008; Suchland, 2011), Jason McGrath's study of Chinese postsocialist culture since the reform era situates postsocialism as 'a global, universally shared condition' (2008: 14). Chinese postsocialism, McGrath argues, is integral to a global framework 'of postsocialist modernity and must be understood in the context of the history of the global capitalist system', as the turn to a market economy has not only reconfigured social processes and cultural production in China, but also altered the trajectory of global capitalism (1–2). More recent scholarship has explored the impact of China's 'neoliberal post-socialism' as 'a deterritorialized form of market post-socialism and a new global system' (Huang, 2020: 2) on the arts and cultures of neighbouring Sinophone territories such as Hong Kong, where spaces for political and cultural intervention have noticeably shrunk since the second postmillennial decade. Claudia Sadowski-Smith and Ioana Luca's concept of 'cultures of global post/socialisms' similarly highlights the expansive latitudes of postsocialism as constituted by a plurality of national and transnational 'spaces, temporalities, and imaginaries' (2022: 426). Such a pluriversal framework reinforces the value of artistic work that can foster dialogues and relational comparisons between Chinese and global postsocialist conditions, and critically reassess both the authoritarian legacies and the progressive potentials of historical experiences of socialism worldwide.

Aesthetic responses to the shifting geopolitics of 'Sinocentric neoliberal post-socialism' (Huang, 2020: 13) in the wider Sinophone region and collaborations between performance makers from China and postsocialist societies in Europe, Asia, and the Global South will thus constitute important transnational dimensions of the performances of Chinese postsocialism to be explored in future research. An equally important area is the growing body of work by international artists from outside the Sinosphere that engages with the global implications of the PRC's economic rise and increasing political clout, pointing to the tangible effects of the current postsocialist moment in the transnational imaginaries of contemporary art and performance. My examination of the entanglements of postsocialist politics, economics, and aesthetics in the so-called Chinese Century therefore concludes with a discussion of the work of American visual artist Jen Liu as a remarkable example of critical engagement with the Chinese postsocialist condition from beyond China's borders.

Liu's artistic research resonates with several of the key issues raised in this study. The futuristic techno-aesthetics of the bio-art project *Pink Slime Caesar Shift* (*PSCS*) incorporate biochemical laboratory tests, live-action and 3D animated video, dance, installation, painting, and sculpture to investigate China's neoliberal labour regime while harnessing the subversive potential of genetic engineering. Similar to Grass Stage's *World Factory* (see Section 3), the works in this series raise issues of labour advocacy, legal rights, occupational safety, and environmental sustainability. Liu specifically addresses racial and gender exploitation in the meat and electronics industries. *PSCS* also draws attention to the toxic cycle – or 'gold loop' – of electronics production, recycling, and chemical extraction of gold microparticles from e-waste after these products are dismantled, often in the same facilities where they were previously assembled, thereby exposing workers to a double risk of industrial poisoning. But industrial meat and gold can also serve as vehicles for speculative resistance, also considering the growing challenges for Chinese labour movements to organise industrial action. Since 2016, Liu has been experimenting with methods of genetic modification, including chemical transfection and gold biolistics, to insert synthetic DNA strands into cow cells that can store coded messages. The modified cells, identifiable by a fluorescent marker, could hypothetically infiltrate the production line via cultivated meat products or be incorporated into wearable sculptures such as rings and bracelets modelled on the antistatic wristbands worn by female factory workers in the electronics industry. These interventions would allow workers to decode embedded data to access vital legal information (encrypted texts include articles from China's Labour Law regulating industrial injuries) and strategies for non-violent protest, connect with activist networks, and coordinate acts of sabotage. The core of the project is therefore not simply a critique of the biopolitical surveillance and the toxic devastation of workers' bodies under conditions of neoliberal excess, but a series of proposals for possible future counteractions through bioactivism.[18]

The meat industry, gendered labour economies, and speculative techno-futures also inform the 2015–16 mixed media series *The Pink Detachment* (video and paintings) and *The Red Detachment of Women* (video and dance performance). This body of work resituates the socialist aesthetic archive within the transnational landscapes of postsocialist globalisation, drawing on organisational and training strategies from the original *yangbanxi* narrative to identify putative solutions to food shortages that ensure both animal welfare and labour justice (Liu, 2016). The single-channel video *The Pink Detachment* blends choreographic performance and 3D animation to transpose the model bodies of the revolutionary ballet from the socialist tropicalism of Hainan Island to the sanitised environment of a meat processing plant. Wu Qinghua, the oppressed peasant-turned-revolutionary soldier, is recast as an alienated worker clumsily attempting to cut up a rack of meat with a knife in a sterile, white-tiled room. The heroic commander Hong Changqing is reimagined as a slick ballerina-manager and paragon of neoliberal efficiency. The manager performs parts of the original choreography in a fluorescent pink room, demonstrating the production-maximising capabilities of a golden meat grinder, just as the communist leader shows the servant girl the path to revolution in the iconic *Red Detachment* scene

[18] For documentation of the artworks and research process, see Liu's website (https://jenliu.info/) and Vimeo channel (https://vimeo.com/user12975947), and Bloomberg Media Studios (2018).

'Changqing Pointing the Way' ('Changqing zhilu'). Thus, the asthetisation of socialist sublimity morphs into the dystopian subalternity of homogenised industrial labour, shifting the ideological thrust of the ballet from the production of human models for the sake of national revolution to the posthuman engineering of national productivity in the service of global capitalism.

The ideological chromaticism of red, for communism, and white, for capitalism, extends to the minced meat and pulverised bones that the grinder – itself colour-coded to signify corporate wealth – mashes up into 'pink slime' (Lean Finely Textured Beef, an additive used in processed meat production), churning out identical pink sausages. Against a pink-saturated backdrop, a squad of worker-dancers, clad in identical overalls, eat evenly sliced pieces of sausage. Reflexively, almost ritualistically, this pink detachment of workers moves in synchrony, like the women soldiers in the model ballet, enacting 'the transformation into a uniform, all-embracing monotechnics', as a female voiceover announces, quoting from Lewis Mumford's *The Myth of the Machine*. A narrative soundtrack that amplifies the colour-coded overlap of ideological and economic models complements the live action and the animated digital rendering of a dystopian techno-pink factory that concludes the video. While revolutionary 'red music' accompanies the manager's re-enactment of the socialist model ballet as a dance of mechanised mass production, in the preceding sequence introducing the meat worker, the voice-over narrator recites a passage from Liu Cixin's 2008 science fiction novel *The Three-Body Problem* (Santi). The text describes the brutal murder of a female Red Guard during the factional violence of the Cultural Revolution. Combined with the ballet's original message of suffering and redemption through revolutionary struggle, the audiovisual layering in this scene seems to imply a substitution of the socialist rhetoric of political martyrdom with the postsocialist logic of inevitable sacrifice, which, as Margaret Hillenbrand writes, justifies 'the subjugation of many millions of the nation's people in a labor regime that grinds and crushes' them like meat and bones: 'The sacrificial class, those whose fingers are lopped off on assembly lines, are also a group whose struggle is narratively consumed by others within a harsh fable of progress' (2023: 130). This is a reversal of what Liu describes as 'the brutal fantasy of the past',[19] into a gendered, neoliberal pink fable. In later scenes, excerpts from various texts, including US federal food safety regulations, intersperse Liu's visual critique of the amalgamation of communism and capitalism in the ideological pink slime of postsocialist neoliberalism. Pink

[19] This and subsequent quotes are taken from the description of *Pink Detachment* published on Liu's website and Vimeo channel. For detailed analysis of Liu's artistic practice, see Bailey (2021).

signifies not only 'a "watered-down" compromise' between economic models and the replacement of 'military overthrow (Red)' with 'manufactured equivalence (Pink)' in the global capitalist system (white), but also 'the pink of femininity [. . .] as a synthetic, potentially violent, hybridity', representing the gendered inequalities of an industrial regime that exploits women's bodies and labour.

Liu's question of whether 'a fraught archival document' can 'be re-motivated, beyond kitsch' – and, one might add, beyond ideology – resonates with the hauntological critique of socialist performance legacies explored in Section 2. Both this and the *PSCS* series echo the documentary testimonies of labour extraction and subaltern exclusion in the dramaturgies of precarity discussed in Section 3 and the themes of speculative futures and technologically induced toxicity examined in Section 4, although toxicity is pathological rather than allegorical in Liu's vision. In essence, Liu's work offers a retro-futurist projection of China's contemporary realities that seamlessly blends the three temporal regimes of postsocialist hauntologies, realisms, and futurities. This brief closing analysis of the American artist's practice proves both uniquely suited to exploring the cross-border convergence of performance and postsocialism, and a fitting conclusion to the exploration of performances of postsocialist times. As not only the temporal regimes, but also the spaces and imaginaries of global postsocialist performance evolve and intertwine, this kind of multidimensional approach forecasts speculative futures for the past and present of Chinese postsocialism, while gesturing towards the expanded future dimensions of performing postsocialism, transnationally.

References

Appadurai, Arjun (2013). *The Future as Cultural Fact: Essays on the Global Condition*. London: Verso.

Atanasoski, Neda, and Kalindi Vora (2018). Postsocialist Politics and the Ends of Revolution. *Social Identities*, 24(2), 139–54.

Baake-Hansen, Martin (2015). Nostalgia and Nostophobia: Emotional Memory in Joseph Roth and Herta Müller. In Devika Sharma, and Frederik Tygstrup, eds., *Structures of Feeling: Affectivity and the Study of Culture*. Berlin: DeGruyter, pp. 116–23.

Bailey, Stephanie (2021). After Communism and Capitalism: On Jen Liu's Political Economy of Matter. *Yishu: Journal of Contemporary Chinese Art*, 20(1), 37–45.

Barlow, Tani (2017). Jiang Qing, Seriously. *The PRC History Review*, 2(4), 1–3.

Baudrillard, Jean (1988). *Selected Writings*. Ed. Mark Poster. Cambridge, MA: Polity Press.

(1998). *The Consumer Society: Myths and Structures*. London: SAGE.

Beijing Contemporary Art Foundation (2020). Mama papa shenghuo jie – Li Jianjun [MamaPapa Festival: Li Jianjun] [Video]. https://youtu.be/d9YgN0fm4o0.

Berry, Chris (2004). *Postsocialist Cinema in Post-Mao China: The Cultural Revolution after the Cultural Revolution*. New York: Routledge.

(2009). Jia Zhangke and the Temporality of Postsocialist Chinese Cinema: In the Now (and Then). In Olivia Khoo, and Sean Metzger, eds., *Futures of Chinese Cinema: Technologies and Temporalities in Chinese Screen Cultures*. Bristol: Intellect, pp. 111–28.

Bleeker, Maaike (2012). Introduction: On Technology & Memory. *Performance Research*, 17(3), 1–7.

Bloomberg Media Studios (2018). [Episode 20] Art + Biochemistry: Jen Liu [Video]. https://vimeo.com/308032460.

Boellstorff, Tom (2014). An Afterword in Four Binarisms. In Mark Grimshaw, ed., *The Oxford Handbook of Virtuality*. New York: Oxford University Press, pp. 739–45.

Boym, Svetlana (2001). *The Future of Nostalgia*. New York: Basic Books.

Browne, Nick (1994). Introduction. In Nick Browne, Paul G. Pickowicz, Vivian Sobchack, and Esther Yau, eds., *New Chinese Cinemas: Forms, Identities, Politics*. Cambridge: Cambridge University Press, pp. 1–12.

Bryant, Rebecca, and Daniel M. Knight (2019). *The Anthropology of the Future*. Cambridge: Cambridge University Press.

Buchanan, Ian (2018). Structure of Feeling. In Ian Buchanan, ed., *A Dictionary of Critical Theory*, 2nd ed. Oxford: Oxford University Press. https://bit.ly/structureoffeeling.

Carlson, Marvin (2001). *The Haunted Stage: The Theatre as Memory Machine*. Ann Arbor: University of Michigan Press.

(2015). Postdramatic Theatre and Postdramatic Performance. *Revista Brasileira de Estudos da Presença*, 5(3), 577–95.

Chekhov, Anton (1983). *Three Sisters*. Trans. Michael Frayn. London: Methuen.

Chun, Tarryn Li-Min (2021). Wang Chong and the Theatre of Im*media*cy: Technology, Performance, and Intimacy in Crisis. *Theatre Survey*, 62(3), 295–321.

Connery, Christopher (2020). World Factory. *Made in China*, 5(1), 136–45.

Derrida, Jacques (2006). *Specters of Marx: The State of Debt, the Work of Mourning and the New International*. Trans. Peggy Kamuf. New York: Routledge.

Ding, Iza (2022). *The Performative State: Public Scrutiny and Environmental Governance in China*. Ithaca, NY: Cornell University Press.

Dirlik, Arif (1989). Postsocialism? Reflections on 'Socialism with Chinese Characteristics'. *Bulletin of Concerned Asian Scholars*, 21(1), 33–44.

Drama Dongcheng [Xiju Dongcheng] (2021). 'Suren juchang' meixue yuyan de shiyan yu tansuo – duihua Li Jianjun daoyan [Experimentation and exploration of the aesthetic language of 'amateur theatre': A conversation with director Li Jianjun] [Video]. https://bit.ly/LJJdramadongcheng.

Elswit, Kate (2018). *Theatre & Dance*. Basingstoke: Palgrave Macmillan.

Erjavec, Aleš (2003). *Postmodernism and the Postsocialist Condition: Politicized Art under Late Socialism*. Berkeley: University of California Press.

Fake Festival [Jia yishu jie] (2020). Dang dianhangong Ma Jiandong zaici zuowei 'yanyuan' taru juchang [When welder Ma Jiandong stepped into the theatre again as an 'actor']. https://bit.ly/LJJfakefestival.

Ferrari, Rossella (2021). Vite postume di un modello. Reincarnazioni postsocialiste del teatro della Rivoluzione Culturale [Afterlives of a model. Postsocialist reincarnations of the theatre of the Cultural Revolution]. *Sinosfere*, 13. https://sinosfere.com/2021/05/23/rossella-ferrari-vite-postume-di-un-modello-reincarnazioni-postsocialiste-del-teatro-della-rivoluzione-culturale/.

(2023). From Realist Drama to Theater of the Real: Postsocialist Realism in Contemporary Chinese Theater. In Jessica Nakamura, and Katherine Saltzman-Li, eds., *Realisms in East Asian Performance*. Ann Arbor: University of Michigan Press, pp. 100–125.

Foucault, Michel (1986). Of Other Spaces. Trans. Jay Miskowiec. *Diacritics*, 16(1), 22–27.

Gao Xingjian (1988). *Dui yi zhong xiandai xiju de zhuiqiu* [In search of modern drama]. Beijing: Zhongguo xiju chubanshe.

Garde, Ulrike, and Meg Mumford (2016). *Theatre of Real People: Diverse Encounters at Berlin's Hebbel am Ufer and Beyond*. London: Bloomsbury.

Gong Baorong (2020). Yuqi genfeng 'juchang', buru jianshou 'xiju' – zai yi postdramatic theater de zhongwen yiming [Sticking to *xiju* rather than following the trend of *juchang*: Reconsidering the Chinese translation of 'postdramatic theatre']. *Xiju yishu* [Theatre arts], 5, 29–39.

Gong Haomin (2012). *Uneven Modernity: Literature, Film, and Intellectual Discourse in Postsocialist China*. Honolulu: University of Hawaii Press.

Grass Stage (2009). *Xiao shehui di yi zhuan* The Little Society 2009 [Video]. https://vimeo.com/209184336.

(2014). *Shijie gongchang* World Factory [Video]. https://vimeo.com/200650753.

Gutman, Yifat, and Jenny Wüstenberg (2023). Introduction: The Activist Turn in Memory Studies. In Yifat Gutman, and Jenny Wüstenberg, eds., *The Routledge Handbook of Memory Activism*. London: Routledge, pp. 5–15.

Harvey, David (1989). *The Condition of Postmodernity: An Enquiry into the Origins of Cultural Change*. Oxford: Blackwell.

Hillenbrand, Margaret (2023). *On the Edge: Feeling Precarious in China*. New York: Columbia University Press.

Hirsch, Marianne (2012). *The Generation of Postmemory: Writing and Visual Culture after the Holocaust*. New York: Columbia University Press.

Huang, Erin Y. (2020). *Urban Horror: Neoliberal Post-Socialism and the Limits of Visibility*. Durham, NC: Duke University Press.

Huyssen, Andreas (1986). *After the Great Divide: Modernism, Mass Culture, Postmodernism*. Bloomington: Indiana University Press.

Jaguścik, Justyna (2022). Rethinking Utopia through Theater: *World Factory* and *The Xiao Ping Incident* by Grass Stage. In Andrea Riemenschnitter, Jessica Imbach, and Justyna Jaguścik, eds., *Sinophone Utopias: Exploring Futures beyond the China Dream*. Amherst, MA: Cambria Press, pp. 225–41.

Jameson, Fredric (1991). *Postmodernism, or, the Cultural Logic of Late Capitalism*. Durham, NC: Duke University Press.

Kattago, Siobhan (2021). Ghostly Pasts and Postponed Futures: The Disorder of Time during the Corona Pandemic. *Memory Studies*, 14(6), 1401–13.

Lanza, Fabio (2023). Always Already and Never Yet: Does China Even Have a Present? *Modern Intellectual History*, 20(2), 601–11.

Lavender, Andy (2019). Reflections upon the ‘Post’: Towards a Cultural History and a Performance-Oriented Perspective. In Peter Eckersall, and Helena Grehan, eds., *The Routledge Companion to Theatre and Politics*. London: Routledge, pp. 9–12.

Lee Kyung-Sung, Boris Nikitin, Wen Hui, Zhao Chuan, and Kai Tuchmann (2022). Shame and Power: A Critical Conversation on the Postdramatic Condition. In Kai Tuchmann, ed., *Postdramatic Dramaturgies: Resonances between Asia and Europe*. Bielefeld: transcript Verlag, pp. 271–86.

Lehmann, Hans-Thies (2006). *Postdramatic Theatre*. Trans. Karen Jürs-Munby. London: Routledge.

(2010). *Houxiju juchang* [Postdramatic theatre]. Trans. Li Yinan. Beijing: Beijing daxue chubanshe.

Li Huizhao (2019). Guandiao pingmu, renlei de lishi jiu zhongjie le! ‘Renlei jianshi’ [Turn off the screen and the history of mankind is over! *A Brief History of Human Evolution*]. *Wuzhen xiju jie tekan* [Wuzhen Theatre Festival special edition], 2, 10.

Li Jianjun (2015). Auf Ruinen Drachen steigen lassen: Die Theatertruppe Neue Jugend und ich/Flying a Kite on Ruins: The New Youth Troupe and I [Bilingual publication]. *Theater der Zeit*, 12, 20–25.

(2019). Guanyu ‘wuming de ren’ de wen yu da [Questions and answers on the ‘nameless mankind’]. In Tian Mansha, and Torsten Jost, eds., *Dangdai Zhongguo daoyan guandian* [Contemporary Chinese perspectives on directing]. Shanghai: Shanghai renmin chubanshe, pp. 207–14.

Li Jie (2020). *Utopian Ruins: A Memorial Museum of the Mao Era*. Durham, NC: Duke University Press.

Li Ning (2010). *Jiaodai* [Tape] [Film]. New York: dGenerate Films.

(2013). Physical Rebels. Trans. Kirk Douglas Kenny. In Jörg Huber, and Zhao Chuan, eds., *The Body at Stake: Experiments in Chinese Contemporary Art and Theatre*. Bielefeld: transcript Verlag, pp. 121–30.

Li Xunnan (2022). How Theatre Is Applied by the Chinese State for Neoliberalism with Chinese Characteristics? The Role of Mass Entrepreneurship and Mass Innovation Policies in a Jingju (Peking opera) Theatre Company. *Research in Drama Education: The Journal of Applied Theatre and Performance*, 27(3), 359–65.

Li Yinan (2019). Leiman de houxiju yu Zhongguo de juchang [Lehmann’s postdramatic theatre and Chinese *juchang*]. *Xiju* [Drama], 4, 48–58.

(2021). *Dangdai juchang fangtanlu: Juchang Performance in Contemporary Chinese Society (1980–2020) Ten Interviews*. Trans. Jo Riley, and Kai Tuchmann. München: utzverlag.

Li Yinan, Boris Nikitin, Wang Mengfan, and Kai Tuchmann (2022). Rethinking Theatricality: A Conversation on Postdramatic Theatre and Chinese *Juchang*. In Kai Tuchmann, ed., *Postdramatic Dramaturgies: Resonances between Asia and Europe*. Bielefeld: transcript Verlag, pp. 33–45.

Li Zheng (2018). Li Ning zhiti juchang chuangzuo fangfa jianxi – yi 'CS–03' wei li [A brief analysis of Li Ning's physical theatre creation method taking *CS-03* as an example]. *Xiju yu yingshi pinglun* [Stage and screen reviews], 6, 59–67.

Liu, Jen (2016). The Red Detachment of Women. *Triple Canopy*, 22. https://canopycanopycanopy.com/contents/the-red-detachment-of-women#fourone.

Lu, Sheldon H. (2007). *Chinese Modernity and Global Biopolitics: Studies in Literature and Visual Culture*. Honolulu: University of Hawai'i Press.

Lyotard, Jean-François (1984). *The Postmodern Condition: A Report on Knowledge*. Trans. Geoff Bennington, and Brian Massumi. Minneapolis: University of Minnesota Press.

Martin, Carol (2013). *Theatre of the Real*. Basingstoke: Palgrave Macmillan.

Massumi, Brian (2014). Envisioning the Virtual. In Mark Grimshaw, ed., *The Oxford Handbook of Virtuality*. New York: Oxford University Press, pp. 55–70.

Mazin, Craig (2018). *Chernobyl* Episode 1 – '1: 23: 45'. https://bit.ly/chernobyl112345.

McGrath, Jason (2008). *Postsocialist Modernity: Chinese Cinema, Literature, and Criticism in the Market Age*. Stanford: Stanford University Press.

(2022). *Chinese Film: Realism and Convention from the Silent Era to the Digital Age*. Minneapolis: University of Minnesota Press.

Miao Ying (2021). Romanticising the Past: Core Socialist Values and the China Dream as Legitimisation Strategy. *Journal of Current Chinese Affairs*, 49(2), 162–84.

New Youth Group (2021). *A Welder's Flash*, by Li Jianjun [Video]. https://vimeo.com/525658267.

Ortells-Nicolau, Xavier (2017). Raised into Ruins: Transforming Debris in Contemporary Photography from China. *Frontiers of Literary Studies in China*, 11(2), 263–97.

Pang Laikwan (2017). *The Art of Cloning: Creative Production during China's Cultural Revolution*. London: Verso.

Parui, Avishek, and Merin Simi Raj (2021). The COVID-19 *Crisis Chronotope*: The Pandemic as Matter, Metaphor and Memory. *Memory Studies*, 14(6), 1431–44.

Pickowicz, Paul G. (1994). Huang Jianxin and the Notion of Postsocialism. In Nick Browne, Paul G. Pickowicz, Vivian Sobchack, and Esther Yau, eds., *New Chinese Cinemas: Forms, Identities, Politics*. Cambridge: Cambridge University Press, pp. 57–87.

Riemenschnitter, Andrea, Jessica Imbach, and Justyna Jaguścik (2022). Introduction: Utopianism across the Sinosphere. In Andrea Riemenschnitter, Jessica Imbach, and Justyna Jaguścik, eds., *Sinophone Utopias: Exploring Futures beyond the China Dream*. Amherst, MA: Cambria Press, pp. 1–20.

Robinson, Luke (2013). *Independent Chinese Documentary: From the Studio to the Street*. Basingstoke: Palgrave Macmillan.

Rojas, Carlos (2016). Introduction: Specters of Marx, Shades of Mao, and the Ghosts of Global Capital. In Carlos Rojas, and Ralph Litzinger, eds., *Ghost Protocol: Development and Displacement in Global China*. Durham, NC: Duke University Press, pp. 1–12.

Sadowski-Smith, Claudia, and Ioana Luca (2022). Introduction: The Cultures of Global Post/Socialisms. *Comparative Literature Studies*, 59(3), 425–46.

Salino, Silvia (2021). Jiang Qing, between Fact and Fiction: The Many Lives of a Revolutionary Icon. *ASIEN*, 158/159, 86–104.

Schechner, Richard (2013). *Performance Studies: An Introduction*, 3rd ed. New York: Routledge.

Seetoo, Chiayi (2021). Documentary in Motion: Dramaturgy of the Corporeal in Chinese Dance Artist Wen Hui's Works. *Asian Theatre Journal*, 38(1), 275–305.

Seetoo, Chiayi, and Haoping Zou (2016). China's Guangchang Wu: The Emergence, Choreography, and Management of Dancing in Public Squares. *TDR: Drama Review*, 60(4), 22–49.

Sohu (2015). Li Jianjun: Xianfeng zhi shi bei tie shang de biaoqian [Li Jianjun: Avant-garde is just a label]. https://bit.ly/LJJSohu2015.

(2017). Yue kuaile, yue jiaolü, women dou shi fanren eryi [The happier we are, the more anxious we are; we are all just human]. https://bit.ly/LJJSohu2017.

Stenning, Alison, and Kathrin Hörschelmann (2008). History, Geography and Difference in the Post-Socialist World: Or, Do We Still Need Post-Socialism? *Antipode*, 40(2), 312–35.

Strauss, Julia C. (2021). Scripts, Authority, and Legitimacy: The View from China and Beyond. In Shirin M. Rai, Milija Gluhovic, Silvija Jestrovic, and Michael Saward, eds., *The Oxford Handbook of Politics and Performance*. Oxford: Oxford University Press, pp. 405–20.

Suchland, Jennifer (2011). Is Postsocialism Transnational? *Signs: Journal of Women in Culture and Society*, 36(4), 837–62.

The Name Time Tries to Erase [Shijian shitu modiao de mingzi] (2018a). Women dui wudao yiwusuozhi [We don't know anything about dance]. https://bit.ly/SewingMachine1.

(2018b). Shanghai 'Shensheng fengrenji' luomu [*The Divine Sewing Machine* ends in Shanghai]. https://bit.ly/SewingMachine2.

Théâtre du Rêve Expérimental (2015). *The Revolutionary Model Play 2.0* – 5 Minute Excerpt [Video]. https://vimeo.com/140903555.

(2019). Wang Chong: *Where Do We Come from, What Are We, Where Are We Going 2.0* [Video]. https://vimeo.com/348157137.

(2020). Online Theater in China [Video]. https://vimeo.com/441938629.

Tilly, Charles (2008). *Contentious Performances*. Cambridge: Cambridge University Press.

Torres, Felipe (2021). *Temporal Regimes: Materiality, Politics, Technology*. New York: Routledge.

Tuchmann, Kai (2022). Introduction. In Kai Tuchmann, ed., *Postdramatic Dramaturgies: Resonances between Asia and Europe*. Bielefeld: transcript Verlag, pp. 3–32.

Wang Chong (2020a). Online Theater Manifesto. www.theatrere.org/online-theater-manifesto-in-english.

(2020b). Xianshang xiju xuanyan [Online theatre manifesto]. www.theatrere.org/online-theater-manifesto.

Wang Mengfan (2020). Yong shenti jinru juchang – cong 'Gai wo shangchang de shihou, jiao wo, wo hui huida' tanqi [Accessing theatre through the body: From *When My Cue Comes, Call Me, and I Will Answer*]. *Xiju yu yingshi pinglun* [Stage and screen reviews], 3, 65–76.

Wang Yin, and Yin Luobi (2005). Guojia xiju zhong de geren fan xiju: fang Zhang Xian [Individual anti-drama within national drama: Interview with Zhang Xian]. *Jintian* [Today], 4, 57–98.

Wei Mei (2021). Vom Tigerberg nach Warschau und Berlin? https://bit.ly/theaterbrief.

Wen Hui (2013). Female Memory Begins with the Body. Trans. Kirk Douglas Kenny. In Jörg Huber, and Zhao Chuan, eds., *The Body at Stake: Experiments in Chinese Contemporary Art and Theatre*. Bielefeld: transcript Verlag, pp. 131–34.

Wen Hui, and Living Dance Studio (2018). *RED* – Wen Hui [Video]. https://youtu.be/Igpds7f1d4M&t=138s.

(2022). RED: A Documentary Performance. Trans. Zhuang Jiayun. In Kai Tuchmann, ed., *Postdramatic Dramaturgies: Resonances between Asia and Europe*. Bielefeld: transcript Verlag, pp. 157–76.

Witke, Roxane (1977). *Comrade Chiang Ch'ing*. Boston, MA: Little, Brown.

Wu Wenguang, ed. (2000). *Xianchang* (1) [Document: 1]. Tianjin: Tianjin shehui kexueyuan chubanshe.

Yan Lianke (2012). *Lenin's Kisses*. Trans. Carlos Rojas. New York: Grove Press.

Zen Experimental Theatre [Zhiren shiyan juchang] (2020). Wang Mengfan: Lai liao 'bu tiaowu de wudao' [Wang Mengfan: Let's talk about 'dance without dancing']. https://bit.ly/wangmengfanZET.

Zhang Xian (2021). Juchang yu wenyi [Theatre and plague]. *Xiju yu yingshi pinglun* [Stage and screen reviews], 1, 52–63.

Zhang Xudong (2008). *Postsocialism and Cultural Politics: China in the Last Decade of the Twentieth Century*. Durham, NC: Duke University Press.

Zhang Yingjin (2007). Rebel without a Cause? China's New Urban Generation and Postsocialist Filmmaking. In Zhang Zhen, ed., *The Urban Generation: Chinese Cinema and Society at the Turn of the Twenty-First Century*. Durham, NC: Duke University Press, pp. 49–80.

Zhang Zhen (2020). Staging the Intimate-Public Camera: Wen Hui's Documentary Practice with Her Third Grandmother. *Studies in Documentary Film*, 14(1), 7–20.

Zhao Chuan (2022). There Is No Empty Space on Earth. In Kai Tuchmann, ed., *Postdramatic Dramaturgies: Resonances between Asia and Europe*. Bielefeld: transcript Verlag, pp. 57–66.

Zhao Chuan, and Grass Stage (2022). World Factory. Trans. Lennet Daigle, and Christopher Connery. In Kai Tuchmann, ed., *Postdramatic Dramaturgies: Resonances between Asia and Europe*. Bielefeld: transcript Verlag, pp. 67–93.

Zhao, Kiki (2016). China's 'Core Socialist Values,' the Song-and-Dance Version. www.nytimes.com/2016/09/02/world/asia/china-dance-socialist-values.html.

Zhuang Jiayun (2017). 'Red': Using the Body to Touch the Contemporaneity of the Past. https://thetheatretimes.com/red-using-body-touch-contemporaneity-past/.

Acknowledgements

I am grateful to Liz Tomlin and Trish Reid for welcoming this project into the series. I thank the anonymous reviewers for their valuable comments and Liz, again, for her generous feedback and thoughtful suggestions. I also thank Fabrizio Massini, Li Yizhuo, and Silvia Salino for stimulating discussions that helped me clarify my thoughts. Fabrizio, particularly, provided crucial assistance in facilitating contacts and sourcing research materials. I am greatly indebted to the artists whose compelling work inspired this research for sharing documentation and granting permission to reproduce text and images. My heartfelt thanks go to the New Youth Group (especially Krista Wang), Wang Chong, Wang Mengfan, Wen Hui, and Zhuang Jiayun. I would also like to acknowledge the financial support of the University of Vienna, which has made it possible to publish this Element as Open Access.

Cambridge Elements ☰

Theatre, Performance and the Political

Trish Reid

University of Reading

Trish Reid is Professor of Theatre and Performance and Head of the School of Arts and Communication Design at the University of Reading. She is the author of *The Theatre of Anthony Neilson* (2017), *Theatre & Scotland* (2013), *Theatre and Performance in Contemporary Scotland* (2024) and co-editor of the *Routledge Companion to Twentieth-Century British Theatre* (2024).

Liz Tomlin

University of Glasgow

Liz Tomlin is Professor of Theatre and Performance at the University of Glasgow. Monographs include *Acts and Apparitions: Discourses on the Real in Performance Practice and Theory* (2013) and *Political Dramaturgies and Theatre Spectatorship: Provocations for Change* (2019). She edited *British Theatre Companies 1995–2014* (2015) and was the writer and co-director with Point Blank Theatre from 1999–2009.

Advisory Board

About the Series

Elements in Theatre, Performance and the Political showcases ground-breaking research that responds urgently and critically to the defining political concerns, and approaches, of our time. International in scope, the series engages with diverse performance histories and intellectual traditions, contesting established histories and providing new critical perspectives.

Cambridge Elements

Theatre, Performance and the Political

Elements in the Series

Theatre Revivals for the Anthropocene
Patrick Lonergan

Re-imagining Independence in Contemporary Greek Theatre and Performance
Philip Hager

Performing Nationalism in Russia
Yana Meerzon

Crisis Theatre and The Living Newspaper
Sarah Jane Mullan and Sarah Bartley

Decolonising African Theatre
Samuel Ravengai

Utpal Dutt and Political Theatre in Postcolonial India
Mallarika Sinha Roy

The Festival of India: Development and Diplomacy at the End of the Cold War
Rashna Darius Nicholson

Theatres of Autofiction
Lianna Mark

Performance and Postsocialism in Postmillennial China
Rossella Ferrari

A full series listing is available at: www.cambridge.org/ETPP

www.ingramcontent.com/pod-product-compliance
Ingram Content Group UK Ltd.
Pitfield, Milton Keynes, MK11 3LW, UK
UKHW022145080726
473066UK00010B/772

* 9 7 8 1 0 0 9 5 1 5 9 4 8 *